RUDIMENTS AND THEORY OF MUSIC

RUDIMENTS AND THEORY OF MUSIC

Based on the Syllabus of the
Theory Examinations of the
Royal Schools of Music

Published by

The Associated Board of the Royal Schools of Music

THE ASSOCIATED BOARD OF THE
ROYAL SCHOOLS OF MUSIC

—

ROYAL ACADEMY OF MUSIC
ROYAL COLLEGE OF MUSIC
ROYAL MANCHESTER
        COLLEGE OF MUSIC
ROYAL SCOTTISH
        ACADEMY OF MUSIC

—

FOR EXAMINATIONS IN MUSIC

—

GREAT BRITAIN, AND NORTHERN IRELAND
EIRE · NEW ZEALAND . SOUTH AFRICA
RHODESIA · KENYA · TANGANYIKA
NYASALAND · GHANA · NIGERIA
MAURITIUS · INDIA · CEYLON · SINGAPORE
MALAYA · HONGKONG · MALTA · CYPRUS
WEST INDIES · BERMUDA

AB 1197

CONTENTS

PREFACE

THIS book on the Rudiments and Theory of Music is laid out on new lines. It follows closely the requirements for each of the eight grades of The Associated Board of the Royal Schools of Music in their examinations on the Theory of Music.

By this method the student will have before him the information that he is likely to require for each grade. It is emphasized that the syllabus is progressive and cumulative from Grade I upwards, and that the student is expected to have knowledge of any subjects specified in preceding grades.

At the end of Grade I and Grade II there is a list of Terms, Signs and Abbreviations which have occurred in the music set in the practical examinations for these grades over a period of years.

At the end of the book there is a list of General Terms which should cover the chief requirements of students in all grades. Furthermore there is a list of Musical Forms, and lastly an exhaustive index designed to give quick reference to any part of the book.

GRADE I (Primary)

THE STAFF (OR STAVE)

1. **Musical sounds** are named, in ascending order, from the first seven letters of the alphabet, A–G, and these are repeated to represent the same notes at higher or lower level.

2. **Octave** (eight) is the term given to the next sound, either above or below, which has the same letter-name, such as A–A, D–D, etc.

3. The word **Pitch** is used to describe how high or how low a sound is, and the pitch of sounds in music is shown by **Notes** (𝅝 𝅗𝅥 𝅘𝅥 𝅘𝅥𝅮 etc.) placed upon the Staff.

4. The **Staff** consists of a series of five parallel lines. Notes can be placed on the lines or in the spaces between the lines. Lines and spaces are always reckoned from the lowest upwards.

lines ——— spaces ———

G AND F CLEFS

5. These notes can have no certain pitch or name until some distinguishing mark is placed at the beginning of the staff.

6. This mark is called a **Clef** (Latin ' clavis,' French ' clef ' meaning a key) and the clef thus becomes the clue to the names of the notes on the Staff.

7. The Treble clef, which was originally a capital G, circles round the second line and fixes that line as G, so that a note on that line represents a sound called G. From this the clef is known not only as Treble clef but as G clef.

NAMES OF NOTES

8. The notes in paragraph 4—undefined as to name and pitch—at once become definite when a clef is placed before them.
Treble Clef.

$$E \quad G \quad B \quad D \quad F \qquad F \quad A \quad C \quad E$$

9. The Bass Clef may be written in two ways :

but whichever form is used, the two dots must be placed on either side of the fourth line so as to fix the pitch of F, from which fact this clef is known as the F clef. The sign itself was in fact originally a capital F.

10. Bass Clef:

$$G \quad B \quad D \quad F \quad A \qquad A \quad C \quad E \quad G$$

11. There is one note which does not appear in the above system of five lines and four spaces, whether in the Treble Clef or the Bass Clef.
That note is ' Middle C,' so called because it is the C nearest to the middle of the piano key-board. It is written on a little line *below* the treble staff or *above* the bass staff.

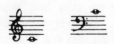

12. Notes in the Treble Clef (with the exception of middle C, which is outside the Staff) will therefore be:

D E F G A B C D E F G

13. Notes in the Bass Clef (with the exception of middle C, which is outside the Staff) will therefore be:

G A B C D E F G A B

14. All the notes so far described are to be found as white keys on the piano or organ.

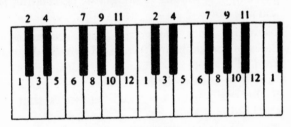

15. The smallest distance between two notes on the key-board is called a **semitone**. There are semitones in the diagram of par. 14 between 1–2, 2–3, 5–6 etc.

16. A **Tone** consists of two semitones, 1–3, 5–7, 9–11, etc.

THE SHARP, FLAT AND NATURAL

17. The **Sharp** (♯) raises a note one semitone in pitch:

D   Dsharp   F   Fsharp

18. The **Flat** (♭) lowers a note one semitone in pitch:

19. The **Natural** (♮) restores the note to its original pitch:

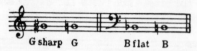

CONSTRUCTION OF THE MAJOR SCALE

20. A **Scale** (*Latin* 'scala' a ladder) is an alphabetical succession of sounds ascending or descending from a starting note.

21. Beginning with the note C, the succeeding white notes of the keyboard form a **Major Scale,** the only kind of scale that we are as yet considering, though as will be discovered later, there are other kinds. It is the position of tones and semitones that decides the kind of scale.

22. The eight notes of the **Major Scale** can be divided into two groups, each containing four notes. Each of these groups is called a **Tetrachord** (Greek tetra = four, chorde = string or note).

It will be seen that in these two tetrachords, the semitones occur in exactly the same place, *i.e.* between the third and the fourth notes. Between all other notes the interval is a tone.

23. The *second* of the two tetrachords above may now be taken to form the *first* or lower tetrachord of a new major scale.
This is done by adding four notes above it:

But it will be seen that, in order to preserve the correct order of tones and semitones, the distance between the third and fourth notes of the second tetrachord should be a semitone, not a tone. To achieve this a sharp (♯) must be placed before the note F to raise it a semitone (te–doh').

24. Thus, in all major scales except C major, there is at least one note which has to be sharpened or flattened whenever it occurs, in order to preserve the correct order of tones and semitones.

25. To sharpen or flatten notes each time they occur would be complicated and confusing, so the sharps or flats are grouped together and written immediately after the clef at the beginning of each line. This indicates the **Key**—the set of notes on which the piece is built, each note having a definite relation to a note known as the key-note. The group of sharps or flats is called the **Key-signature.**

26. Any sharps or flats occurring in the course of a piece other than those in the key-signature are called **Accidentals.**

27. The scale of G Major may therefore be written with its key-signature :

28. Examination candidates are sometimes asked to write
a scale *without* key-signature. In this case write out
the notes of the scale required (*e.g.* D major) and put
accidentals before those notes which require them:

29. Similarly in the scale of D Major *with* key-signature,
the correct order of tones and semitones would be :

30. The scale of F major *without* key-signature:

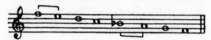

The scale of F major *with* key-signature:

TONIC TRIADS (IN ROOT POSITION IN THE
MAJOR KEYS OF C G D F)

31. The **tonic** is the key-note.
The tonic triad in a major key is a chord of three
notes, consisting of the tonic, third and fifth of the
scale (doh–me–soh).
Tonic triad of C major:

32. It will be noticed that if the tonic (or key-note) is on a line, the two remaining notes will be on the next two lines above; similarly, if the tonic is a space, the two remaining notes will occupy the two spaces immediately above the key-note:

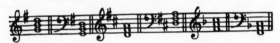

TIME VALUES OF NOTES
DOTTED NOTES AND RESTS

33. The length (or duration) of sounds is shown by Notes of different shapes (see Grade I, 3). Periods of silence are shown by signs called **Rests**.

Note	Shape	Rest	Value in terms of a Semibreve	Corresponding names used in U.S.A. and Canada
Semibreve	𝅝	𝄻	1	Whole Note
Minim	𝅗𝅥	𝄼	$\frac{1}{2}$	Half Note
Crotchet	𝅘𝅥	𝄽 or 𝄽	$\frac{1}{4}$	Quarter Note
Quaver	𝅘𝅥𝅮	𝄾	$\frac{1}{8}$	Eighth Note
Semiquaver	𝅘𝅥𝅯	𝄿	$\frac{1}{16}$	Sixteenth Note
Demisemiquaver	𝅘𝅥𝅰	𝅀	$\frac{1}{32}$	Thirty-second Note

N.B. A Breve ⫢ is twice as long as a Semibreve, and its rest is ⫢

It is seldom found now except in old music.

34. Table showing the number of notes contained in one semibreve:

1 Semibreve	𝅝
2 Minims	𝅗𝅥 𝅗𝅥
4 Crotchets	𝅘𝅥 𝅘𝅥 𝅘𝅥 𝅘𝅥
8 Quavers	𝅘𝅥𝅮 𝅘𝅥𝅮 𝅘𝅥𝅮 𝅘𝅥𝅮 𝅘𝅥𝅮 𝅘𝅥𝅮 𝅘𝅥𝅮 𝅘𝅥𝅮
16 Semiquavers	𝅘𝅥𝅯𝅘𝅥𝅯𝅘𝅥𝅯𝅘𝅥𝅯 𝅘𝅥𝅯𝅘𝅥𝅯𝅘𝅥𝅯𝅘𝅥𝅯 𝅘𝅥𝅯𝅘𝅥𝅯𝅘𝅥𝅯𝅘𝅥𝅯 𝅘𝅥𝅯𝅘𝅥𝅯𝅘𝅥𝅯𝅘𝅥𝅯
32 Demisemiquavers	𝅘𝅥𝅰𝅘𝅥𝅰𝅘𝅥𝅰𝅘𝅥𝅰𝅘𝅥𝅰𝅘𝅥𝅰𝅘𝅥𝅰𝅘𝅥𝅰 𝅘𝅥𝅰𝅘𝅥𝅰𝅘𝅥𝅰𝅘𝅥𝅰𝅘𝅥𝅰𝅘𝅥𝅰𝅘𝅥𝅰𝅘𝅥𝅰 𝅘𝅥𝅰𝅘𝅥𝅰𝅘𝅥𝅰𝅘𝅥𝅰𝅘𝅥𝅰𝅘𝅥𝅰𝅘𝅥𝅰𝅘𝅥𝅰 𝅘𝅥𝅰𝅘𝅥𝅰𝅘𝅥𝅰𝅘𝅥𝅰𝅘𝅥𝅰𝅘𝅥𝅰𝅘𝅥𝅰𝅘𝅥𝅰

35. In listening to music it will be noticed that there is a steady throb to which one could clap. This is called the **Pulse** or **Beat.**

36. Some beats or pulses will be stronger than others; and are called **Accents.**

37. The beats usually fall into regular groups of two or three, the first of each group being an accent.

38. The number of beats from one accent to another divides the music into equal measures, each of which is called a **Bar.**

39. In order to show where these divisions come, a line called a **Bar-line** is placed across the stave.

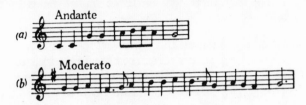

The tune at (*a*) will therefore be in two time. and that at (*b*) will be in three time.

40. At the end of a piece of music, or a section of a piece, two bar-lines are placed across the stave. This is called a **Double Bar**.

41. The time of a piece of music is shown by the **Time-signature,** and this is placed immediately after the key-signature at the beginning of the piece.

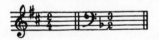

42. It will be seen from the above that the Time-signature consists of two figures placed one above the other. For the present it will be sufficient to regard the upper figure as showing how many beats there are in a bar, and the lower figure the value of each beat.

Thus, $\frac{2}{4}$ indicates that there are to be two Crotchet beats (or Quarter-notes, see paragraph 33) in each bar. Similarly $\frac{3}{2}$ means that there will be three Minim beats (or Half-notes) in each bar.

43. Thus, in the two examples in paragraph 41, $\frac{2}{4}$ indicates that there will be two crotchet beats in each bar, and $\frac{3}{2}$ that there will be three minim beats in each bar.

44. Similarly, $\frac{3}{8}$ means three quaver beats in a bar
$\frac{3}{4}$ means three crotchet beats in a bar
$\frac{4}{4}$ means four crotchet beats in a bar
$\frac{2}{2}$ means two minim beats in a bar

45. $\frac{4}{4}$ time is sometimes (often in old music) called **Common Time,** and instead of figures ($\frac{4}{4}$) it is shown by the sign C. It should be pointed out that C is not a capital letter for Common Time. In early days music in three time was represented by O, the circle or symbol of perfection ; music in two or four time by C, the imperfect or incomplete circle.

46. $\frac{2}{2}$ time is often called **Alla Breve**, and is shown by the sign ₵

47. Students are advised not to use the signs C or ₵ (though their meaning should be known) for they are apt to lead to confusion.

There can, however, be no doubt about :
$\frac{4}{4}$ (four crotchet beats in a bar)
$\frac{2}{2}$ (two minim beats in a bar)
$\frac{4}{2}$ (four minim beats in a bar)

DOTTED NOTES AND RESTS

48. The value of a note or rest can be increased by placing a dot after it.

The effect of the dot is to increase the length of the note or rest by half its original value.

49. Thus, ♩. or ៵· is equal to the value of 3 quavers.

    ♪. or ៵· is equal to the value of 3 semiquavers.

50. The value of a note may also be increased:

  (1) By a **Tie** or Bind. ♩‿♪ = a crotchet plus a quaver. The first note only is sounded, but it is held on for its own length plus that of the following tied note.

  (2) By placing *two* dots after the original note: ♩.. The effect of the first dot is to increase the value of the note by half, and the second dot adds again half the value of the first dot.

Thus, (1) ♩. = ♩‿♪ = 3 quavers.

    (2) ♩.. = ♩‿♪‿♪ = 3 quavers plus 1 semiquaver, or 7 semiquavers.

51. Table showing Simple Time Signatures : that is, Time-signatures in which the beat is of the value of an ordinary note (minim, crotchet etc.).   Other beat-values will be met later on.

Simple Duple 2 beats in a bar	Simple Triple 3 beats in a bar	Simple Quadruple 4 beats in a bar
$\frac{2}{2}$ ♩ ♩	$\frac{3}{2}$ ♩ ♩ ♩	$\frac{4}{2}$ ♩ ♩ ♩ ♩
$\frac{2}{4}$ ♩ ♩	$\frac{3}{4}$ ♩ ♩ ♩	$\frac{4}{4}$ ♩ ♩ ♩ ♩
$\frac{2}{8}$ ♪ ♪	$\frac{3}{8}$ ♪ ♪ ♪	$\frac{4}{8}$ ♪ ♪ ♪ ♪

TO FIND THE KEY OF A MELODY

52. If the passage contains sharp accidentals only, find which sharp is the last in key-signature order.

53. The order of sharps (two for this Grade) is as follows:

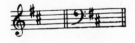

54. The last sharp is always the seventh degree of the scale; therefore, the key-note will be a semitone above.

The last sharp in order in the above tune (see paragraph 53) is C sharp; therefore the key-note (a semitone above) will be D, and the key D major, because of the presence of F sharp in the tune.

55. If a passage contains flats only (there is only one flat key in this Grade) the key-note will be four notes below this flat.

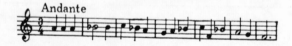

The flat is B flat, therefore the key will be F major.

Warning. A tune does not necessarily begin or end on the key-note. The tune in paragraph 54 does neither. The tune in paragraph 55 ends on the key-note, but does not begin on it.

TERMS AND SIGNS

Students should have a knowledge of simple Italian words, abbreviations and signs that are likely to be found in the music set for Grade I.

In the list which follows, an endeavour has been made to include all signs and terms which have occurred in the music set for Grade I over a period of years.

A tempo	Resume the normal speed (after a diversion)
Accelerando accel.	} Becoming gradually faster
Adagio	Slow, leisurely
Allargando	Broadening out, often with an increase of tone
Allegretto	(*lit.* a little allegro) Slightly slower than Allegro
Allegro .	Lively, reasonably fast.
Andante	(*lit.* walking) At a moderate pace
Andantino	(*lit.* a little andante) This word has two opposite meanings; either a little slower or a little faster than Andante
Arco	(for string players) With the bow; a contradiction of *pizzicato*
Brillante	Sparkling, brilliant
Brio	Vigour
Cantabile	In a singing style
Capo	(*lit.* head) The beginning
Col, Colla	With the
Con	With
Con moto	With movement
Con sordini	With the mutes (see sordini)

Corda	. . .	A string (see una corda, tre corde)
Crescendo Cresc.	. .	Becoming gradually louder
Da	. . .	From, of
Da Capo D.C.	. .	From the beginning
Dal Segno	. .	From the sign 𝄋
Decrescendo	.	Becoming gradually softer
Diminuendo Dim.	. .	Becoming gradually softer
Dolce	. . .	Sweetly
Espressivo Espress.	. .	With expression, with feeling
Fine	. . .	The end [D.C. al Fine; back to the beginning and finish at the word Fine]
Forte *f*	. . .	Loud
Fortissimo *ff*	. . .	Very loud
Forzando *fz* or *sfz*	. .	With a strong accent
Giocoso	. . .	Gay, merry
Grave	. . .	Very slow
Grazioso	.	Gracefully
Largo	. . .	Slow and stately, broad
Larghetto	. .	Less slow than Largo
Legato	. . .	Smoothly
Leggiero	. .	Lightly
Lento	. . .	Slowly
Maestoso	. .	Majestically
M.D. (It.) Mano destra.	. .	Right hand

M.S. (It.) Mano sinistra	. .	Left hand
Marcato	. .	Marked, accented
Meno	. .	Less
Meno mosso	. .	Less movement
Mezzo forte} *mf*	.	Moderately loud
Mezzo piano} *mp*	.	Moderately soft
Misterioso	. .	Mysteriously
Molto	. .	Much
Ossia	. .	Or. The word indicates an alternative version
Ped.	. .	Depress the sustaining pedal of the pianoforte
Perdendosi	. .	Dying away
Pesante	. .	Heavily
Piacevole	. .	Pleasing
Pianissimo} *pp*	.	Very soft
Piano} *p*	. .	Soft
Pizzicato} Pizz.	.	Plucked (in string music)
Più	. .	More
Poco	. .	A little
Poco a poco	.	Little by little (gradually)
Presto	. .	Very quick
Prestissimo	.	As fast as possible
Rallentando} Rall.	.	Becoming gradually slower
Risoluto	.	Boldly
Ritardando} Ritard	.	Becoming gradually slower
Ritenuto (rit.)	.	Hold back (i.e. slower at once)

Ritmico	. .	Rhythmically
Scherzo	. .	A joke
Scherzando	. .	Playfully
Segno .	. .	A sign 𝄉 (see dal segno)
Sempre .	. .	Always
Senza .	. .	Without
Sforzando *sf* or *sfz* }	. .	With a sudden accent
Simile .	. .	In a similar manner
Sordini .	. .	Mutes. Con sordini: with mutes, a direction for string or brass players. Senza sordini: without mutes
Staccato Stacc. }	. .	Short, detached
Stringendo	. .	Gradually faster
Subito .	. .	Suddenly
Tempo .	. .	The speed of the music.
Tempo di Gavotta	.	In the time (and style) of a Gavotte
Tempo Primo Tempo I }	.	Resume the original speed
Tenuto Ten. }	. .	Held
Tranquillo	. .	Quietly
Tre corde	. .	(*lit.* Three strings) Release the left (soft) pedal of the pianoforte
Troppo .	. .	Too much
Una corda	. .	(*lit.* One string) Depress the left (soft) pedal of the pianoforte
Vivace .	. .	Lively, quick

SIGNS

>	Accent
⌒	Slur (smooth)
♩ = 88	88 crotchets to the minute
< >	Getting louder, then softer
♩ ♩	Staccato dots
♪ (Acciaccatura or crushing note)	An extra note played as quickly as possible *on* the beat, not before it
⌢	Phrase mark
♩ ♫	Tie or bind
♩	Give prominence
⌒	Pause
Ped. or Ped_____| or Ped. *	Depress sustaining pedal, then release
|| : : ||	The passage is to be repeated
| ♩ ♩ | ♩ ♩ | ♩ ||	Bar lines and Double Bar
V For String Players	Up bow
⊓ „ „ „	Down bow

GRADE II (Elementary)

1. It has already been seen (Grade I, par. 11) that middle C has no place on either Treble or Bass stave, but has to be written on a little extra line below the Treble or above the Bass. This fact led many people to imagine that this little line was really part of the middle line of an eleven-line stave, which they called the Great Stave. This is not, in fact, historically correct. There has never been an an eleven line stave.

LEGER LINES

2. The little line on which middle C is written is called a leger line.

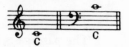

Leger lines are used whenever the note is too high or too low to be written on the staff.

As many leger lines can be used as are required. For instance, the scale of F can be continued above the treble staff or below the bass staff:

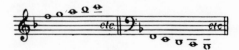

It is often found convenient to write leger lines **above** the bass even for notes which can be written **on the** treble staff: or similarly to write leger lines below the treble which could be written on the bass staff.

instead of

In order to avoid the trouble of writing (and reading) too many leger lines, music is sometimes written an octave lower or an octave higher than it is intended to be played. This is shown by a figure 8 with **a** dotted line over or under the passage in question.

PROKOFIEV
Classical Symphony

Molto vivace

(a)

(by permission,
Boosey &
Hawkes)

DEBUSSY
La Cathédrale Engloutie

(b)   Con moto

(by permission,
Durand Paris)

SCALES

3. The scale of A major.

The two sharps which belong to D major remain. The new sharp is G sharp, the seventh note of the scale (te).

The key signature has three sharps which are grouped as follows:

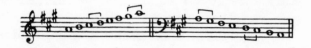

CONSTRUCTION OF THE MINOR SCALE

4. The scale of A minor.
If we write the last three notes of the scale of C major, ABC (lah te doh'), we have the first three notes of the scale known as A minor. The semitone from B to C now comes between the second and third notes.

Continue this to complete the tetrachord and we have ABCD.

Now compare this with the scale of A major.

One note is different—the third. It is this third note which really decides whether a scale is major or minor.

The distance from the first to the third note in the major scale is a semitone greater than in the minor scale (A to C sharp is a greater distance than A to C natural).

The word 'major' means 'greater' and the word 'minor' means 'smaller.' In fact at one time composers referred to the key of A with the greater third or the key of A with the lesser third.

5. It now remains to complete the scale of A minor by adding the upper tetrachord.

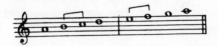

It is necessary here again to sharpen the seventh note, in order to make a semitone from the seventh to the eighth note.

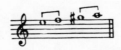

This makes a rather big step from the sixth to the seventh, F natural to G sharp, but both these notes are necessary in constructing the harmony of A minor, and from that fact this scale is called the **harmonic** minor scale.

6. There is, however, another way of writing the upper tetrachord of a minor scale. Here the sixth note is sharpened as well as the seventh, and it will be found that the effect is smoother than in the harmonic form of the scale.

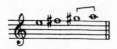

But, in coming down, these sharps have to be changed to naturals if the same smooth effect is to remain:

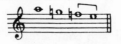

This form of the minor scale, being more melodious and easier to sing than the harmonic form, is called the **melodic** minor scale.

7. Now compare the complete scale of A minor harmonic with that of A minor melodic:

Harmonic

Melodic

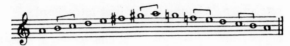

Notice that the harmonic form is the same both up and down, but that the melodic form, is different in the two directions.

8. The scale of A minor has no sharps or flats in its key signature, but in this and in all minor scales the sharpened seventh in the harmonic form and the sharpened sixth and seventh in the melodic form of the scale are indicated by accidentals written against them.

9. The scales of C major and A minor have the same key signature. For this reason they are said to be related to each other. C major is the relative major of A minor and A minor is the relative minor of C major.

To find the key-note of the relative minor of any major key remember that the last three notes of a major scale (lah te doh¹) form the first three notes of its relative minor.

The key-note of the relative major of a minor key is the third note of the minor scale.

10. The scale of E minor harmonic.
Write the first three notes E F sharp and G, a tone and a semitone, exactly as in A minor (see par. 4).

G is then the relative major with key signature of one sharp. Complete the first tetrachord:

Now complete the scale by adding the upper tetrachord with the seventh note sharpened:

11. The scale of E minor melodic.

The lower tetrachord is the same as in the harmonic form. Add the upper tetrachord with the sixth and seventh notes sharpened:

ascending

Now to make the descending form of the melodic minor, contradict the sharps of both 7th and 6th degrees with naturals:

descending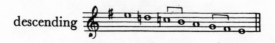

12. The scale of D minor harmonic:

F is the relative major with key signature of one flat. Complete the first tetrachord:

Now complete the scale by adding the upper tetrachord with the seventh note sharpened:

13. The scale of D minor melodic.

The first tetrachord is the same. In the upper tetrachord the sixth note must be raised and becomes B natural. The seventh is C sharp:

ascending   

In descending the sixth and seventh must be flattened, B natural becoming B flat and C sharp becoming C natural:

descending   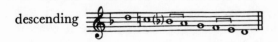

TONIC TRIADS

14. Notice that the tonic triad of A major has C sharp as its middle note:

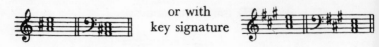

or with
key signature

Triads in a minor key are formed in the same way as in a major key:

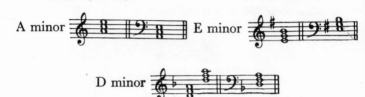

A minor   E minor

D minor

TO FIND THE KEY OF A MELODY

For general information and the keys of C, G, D and F, see Grade I, 52–55.

15. A knowledge of the scales is essential. The scale of A major is already known and its key can be easily recognized by the presence of its seventh note, the last sharp, G sharp.

Allegretto   SCHUBERT
                             Piano Sonata

The last sharp in key-signature order, in the above melody is G sharp, therefore the keynote will be A. The other sharps, F and C, make it clear that the key is A major.

Minor Keys

16. In a minor key the seventh note of the scale (ascending) is also the 'sharpest' note.

When the seventh has been found, it is best to look next for the third of the scale.

Here the G sharp establishes the key of A, but the presence of C natural and F natural instead of C sharp and F sharp shows it to be A minor.

Melodies in a minor key may contain accidentals from all forms of the minor scale both harmonic and melodic.

Notice that a melody need not begin or end on the tonic.

INTERVALS

17. An interval in music is the distance in pitch from one note to another. Intervals are measured by the number of letter names from the lower note to the upper, both of which are included in the count.

Thus, from C to D there are only two letter names included. This is, therefore, an interval of a second. From C to E includes three letter names (C, D, E). This is, therefore, an interval of a third. From C to F is a fourth and from C to G a fifth.

18. When the two notes which form an interval both belong to the same key and can be found in its scale, the interval is said to be **diatonic.**

19. The words ' major ' and ' minor ' are already known in connection with scales. They are also used to describe different kinds of intervals. For instance, the diatonic interval of a tone (C to D) is called a **major** second, and the diatonic interval of a semitone (E to F) is called a **minor** second.

    Intervals of a third are also described as major or minor. From C to E is a major third and from A to C is a minor third.

    It can be seen that a major third contains two tones and a minor third a tone and a semitone.

20. Intervals of a fourth (C to F) and of a fifth (C to G) are described as **perfect** intervals. There is no such thing as a major or minor fourth or fifth.

21. Diatonic intervals from the tonic up to the fifth in the scale of C major:

The order is the same from the tonic in all major scales: Major 2nd, major 3rd, perfect 4th, perfect 5th.

22. Intervals from the tonic up to the fifth in the scale of A minor:

The order is the same from the tonic to the fifth in all minor scales: major 2nd, minor 3rd, perfect 4th, perfect 5th.

⁶⁄₈ TIME

23. In ²⁄₄ time (Simple Duple) each beat can be divided into two quavers ²⁄₄ ♫ ♫ There is also another kind of duple time in which the beats are divided into three quavers ♫♫ ♫♫ Here there is a total of six quavers and the time signature is ⁶⁄₈.

Although there are six quavers there are only two main beats. These are written as dotted crotchets ♩. ♩. each comprising three quavers.

⁶⁄₈ time is called compound time because a bar is made up of a mixture (or compound) of two and three. Each bar has two main beats ♩. ♩. and each of these has three subdivisions ♫♫ ♫♫

24. In writing in compound duple time it is necessary to group the notes so that the division at the half bar shall be clear and each of the main beats complete in itself. ⁶⁄₈ ♩ ♪ ♫♫ | ♩. ♩. ‖

This grouping is also necessary in order to avoid confusion with ³⁄₄ time. Compare the following:

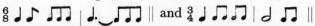

The note values are the same but the grouping is different: so indeed is the rhythmic effect.

Nevertheless a single sound to fill a whole bar will be written ♩. in both ³⁄₄ and ⁶⁄₈.

25. When rests are to be written, grouping in beats will
still be normal.

When rests follow notes the rule is to add such a
rest as will complete the whole note, first completing the value of the half note if necessary, and then
a further rest for the dot : e.g. ⁶⁄₈ ♪ 𝄾 𝄾 not ♪ 𝄾 : the
dot in fact must be represented by a separate rest :
so—⁶⁄₈ ♪ 𝄾 𝄾 𝄾 𝄾 𝄾 |

TRIPLETS

26. Sometimes composers write three notes in the place
of two, as if a beat of ⁶⁄₈ time had found its way into a
bar of ²⁄₄ time.

The three notes form what is known as a triplet and
are grouped together with a figure 3 written against
them.

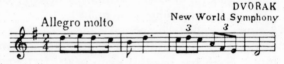

DVOŘAK
New World Symphony
Allegro molto

Here it is a crotchet beat divided into three quavers,
but it is equally possible to have a minim beat divided
in a similar way into three crotchets : ²⁄₂ 𝅗𝅥 𝅘𝅥 𝅘𝅥 𝅘𝅥 |

BARRING AN UNBARRED PHRASE

27. Whether the question is to add bar lines or to add a
time-signature, it is important that the rhythm and
pulse of the melody shall be felt and understood.
An attempt may first be made to tap the rhythm of
the phrase, feeling the regular beat of the pulse and
also trying to feel where the strongest accents occur.
In this way a rough estimate of the correct answers
can be quickly reached.

The answers can then be checked by the following methods.

28. If bar lines are to be added to a phrase of which the time signature is given, it is obvious that time signatures must be known and understood.

Everything then depends on an exact knowledge of note values.

In this Grade the phrase will probably begin on the first beat of the bar. The crotchets, quavers, rests, dotted notes, etc., can be counted from the beginning to make up the number of beats for the first bar according to the time signature.

Then the next bar is counted out in the same way, and so on until all the bars of the phrase are complete.

29. When bar lines are given and the time signature is required to be added, it is necessary first to find out how many beats in a bar there are.

First notice how the quavers and small notes are grouped,

whether in twos

or in threes

If they are grouped in twos the time is Simple, but if in threes, the time so far as this Grade is concerned will be Compound Duple and the time signature will be $\frac{6}{8}$.

If the phrase is in Simple time it may be Duple, Triple, or Quadruple.

The total number of notes and rests in each bar will add up in value to a multiple of either two or three.

If two is the answer, the time signature will be $\frac{2}{4}$, or $\frac{4}{4}$, or perhaps $\frac{4}{2}$. The total value of notes and rests will decide this

If three is the answer the time signature will be
$\frac{3}{8}$, $\frac{3}{4}$, or $\frac{3}{2}$ according to the total value of notes and
rests, but be sure that you are clear that it is Simple
time.

RHYTHM OF MUSICAL PHRASES IN RELATION TO WORDS

30. Language has its own natural rhythm. The words
and syllables when spoken form themselves into
rhythmic groups of two, three or four. The rhythm
of words can be made to fit into a musical phrase.
Consider the words, ' Baa, baa, black sheep, have
you any wool? '
They at once form themselves into a rhythm which
can be written down in musical notation.

' Baa, baa, black sheep, have you any wool? '

The rhythm is suggested by the accents which fall on
the important words or syllables in the sentence.
These must be placed on the first beat of a bar.
If the accents are felt on the first beat of each bar
it is obvious that the following setting is wrong:

' Baa baa black sheep have you an-y wool? '

A musical phrase is commonly, but not invariably
four bars in length. If the words 'have you any '
in the first example were set to crotchets instead of
quavers, the phrase would be five bars long and the
rhythmic balance might be spoilt.

31. Now, take the words ' Little Jack Horner sat in the
corner.' First count the total number of syllables in
the sentence. There are ten, and each will have to
have a note.

Now write accents over the important syllables:

   >   >   >   >

' Little Jack Horner sat in the corner.'

Do the words form themselves into groups of two or three syllables?

The answer is both!   3 2 3 2.

In crotchets it would be

♩ ♩ ♩ | ♩ ♩ | ♩ ♩ ♩ | ♩ ♩ ‖
' Little Jack Horner sat in the corner.'

To get a time signature we must make up the *two* beats to the value of three by using longer notes for *Horner* and *corner*.

$\frac{3}{4}$ ♩♩ ♩ | ♩ ♩ | ♩ ♩ ♩ | ♩♩ ‖
' Little Jack Horner sat in the corner.'

Another way of doing it would be to *shorten* the syllables of ' little ' and ' in the,' making them quavers and the time signature $\frac{2}{4}$

$\frac{2}{4}$ ♪♪ ♩ ♩ | ♩ ♩ | ♩ ♪ ♪ | ♩ ♩ ‖
' Little Jack Horner sat in the corner.'

In each case the accents are still on the first beat of the bar though the rhythmic effect is different.

Sometimes the sentence is much longer, but it can still be made to fit into four bars if the rhythm of the words is allowed to flow naturally.

' Yesterday upon the stair I met a man who wasn't there.'

$\frac{6}{8}$ ♪♪ ♩ ♪| ♩♪ ♩♪| ♩♪ ♩ ♪| ♩♪ ♩.|
' Yesterday up-on the stair I met a man who wasn't there.'

Sometimes candidates are asked: ' Which of these rhythms is the more suitable to the words, and why? '

(a)
The Queen of Hearts she made some tarts, all on a summer's day

(b)
The Queen of Hearts she made some tarts, all on a summer's day

The second (b) is the more suitable because the important words are made to fall on the accented beats. The phrase is four bars in length and the rhythmic flow of the words is maintained.

Objections to (a):

1. The natural rhythm of the words is not preserved.

2. The accents which should fall on the important words are not on the first beat of the bar. See the words, ' The,' ' Hearts,' ' some,' ' on.'

TERMS

Affrettando	. .	Hurrying
Agitato .	. .	Agitated
Alla	. .	In the style of
Alla breve	. .	$\frac{2}{2}$ or $\frac{4}{2}$ time; also expressed by ₵
Alla marcia	. .	In the style of a March
Alla Polacca .	. .	In the style of a Polonaise
Attacca .	. .	Go on immediately
Calando	. .	Softer and slower by degrees
Forza	. .	Force, power
Fuoco	. .	Fire,
Giusto .	. .	Exact, strict (tempo giusto = in strict time)
Largamente .	. .	In a broad style
Mesto	. .	Sad
Mezzo .	. .	Half

Moderato . .	At a moderate pace
Morendo . .	Dying away
Mosso⎫ Moto ⎭ . .	Motion, movement
Non . . .	Not (Allegro non troppo = not too fast)
Seconda volta .	Second time
Slargando⎫ Slentando⎭ .	Gradually slower
Smorzando . .	Dying away
Sostenuto . .	Sustained
Spirito .. .	Spirit, life, energy
Spiritoso . .	Lively, animated
Strepitoso . .	Noisy, boisterous
Tacet . . .	Silent
Volti subito⎫ V.S. ⎭ .	Turn the page quickly

GRADE III (Transitional)

MAJOR SCALES OF E, B FLAT, E FLAT, A FLAT

1. The scale of E major.
   The new sharp in this key is D sharp, and comes on
   the seventh note of the scale to make the semitone
   (te-doh¹).

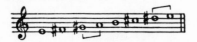

2. The key-signature has four sharps:

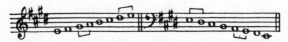

3. Notice that in all major keys which have sharps in
   the key-signature, the last sharp is always the seventh
   degree of the scale (te) and it is thus an easy matter
   to find the key-note (doh).

4. The scale of B flat major.
   The new flat in this key is E flat and is necessary in
   order that the semitone in the first tetrachord should
   occur (as in all major scales) between the third and
   fourth degrees of the scale.

5. The key-signature has two flats:

6. Notice that in all major keys which have flats in the key-signature, the last flat is always a fourth above (or a fifth below) the key-note.

7. The scale of E flat major. Key-signature three flats
   The new flat in this key is A flat.

8. The scale of A flat major. Key-signature four flats
   The new flat in this key is D flat.

HARMONIC AND MELODIC MINOR SCALES
OF G AND C

9. The construction of the minor scale (in both forms) has already been described in Grade II (4–13) and the procedure is the same for all keys.

10. The scale of G minor. Key-signature two flats. Relative major B♭

Harmonic

Melodic

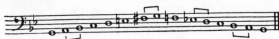

11. The scale of C minor.   Key-signature three flats.
    Relative major E♭

Harmonic

Melodic

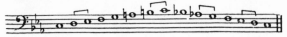

12. Table showing key-signatures and tonic triads, in
    root and close position of the keys specified for Grade
    III.

E major

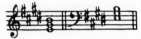

B♭ major

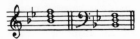

E♭ major

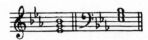

A♭ major

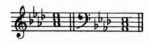

G minor

C minor

DIATONIC INTERVALS IN THE NINE SPECIFIED MAJOR KEYS FROM THE TONIC UPWARDS

13. Diatonic intervals in **major** scales (from the tonic up to the fifth) have been described in Grade II, 21. The remaining three intervals can now be added, so as to include all diatonic intervals from key-note to key-note (doh-doh').

C major

Major   Major   Perfect
6th   7th   8th(octave)

14. The order is the same in **all major keys** from tonic to tonic (doh-doh').

C major

2nd 3rd 4th 5th 6th 7th 8th

Major Major Perfect Perfect Major Major Perfect

15. Further examples:

E major

Major Major Perfect Perfect Major Major Perfect

A♭ major

Major Major Perfect Perfect Major Major Perfect

16. Diatonic intervals in minor scales from the tonic up to
the fifth have been described in Grade II, 22.
The order is the same in **all minor keys** from the
tonic up to the fifth (doh-soh).

17. Examples in the keys of G minor and C minor:

G minor

Major Minor Perfect Perfect

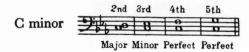

C minor

Major Minor Perfect Perfect

COMPOUND DUPLE TIME

18. Besides the compound duple time ($\frac{6}{8}$) described in
Grade II, 23, the following forms should also be
known :

19. $\frac{6}{4}$ time. The beat is a dotted minim:

20. Quavers and notes of smaller value, should be correctly grouped. The note lengths used should show the division of the bar into *two* beats, but subject to a few exceptions noted in par. 23.

The total value of (*a*) and (*b*) is the same, but the rhythmical effect is quite different in that (*a*) is in $\frac{6}{4}$, the bar being clearly divided into two equal halves, but (*b*) is in $\frac{3}{2}$ showing by the arrangement of the notes a clear division into three minim beats.

21. $\frac{6}{16}$ time. The beat is a dotted quaver:

and the correct grouping of a passage in $\frac{6}{16}$ time would be:

GROUPING OF NOTES AND RESTS

22. In order to help the eye in reading music and to show more clearly the sub-divisions of the bar, quavers and notes of lesser value are grouped together.

For instance, $\frac{4}{4}$ ♩♩ ♪♪♪♪ ♩♪ ♪♩ ‖

is much easier to read than

$\frac{4}{4}$ ♪ ♪ ♪ ♪ ♪ ♪ ♪ ♪ ♪ ♪ ♪ ♪

23. The rule is: Group together as many notes as make one beat.

Exceptions:

(a) In a bar of $\frac{4}{4}$ time, if the first two or the last two beats consist of quavers, they should be grouped together:

(b) The four quavers in a bar of $\frac{2}{4}$ time should be similarly grouped:

(c) If a bar of $\frac{3}{4}$ or $\frac{3}{8}$ time consists entirely of quavers, or a bar of $\frac{3}{8}$ time entirely of semiquavers, then all the notes should be grouped together:

N.B. In setting words to music these conventions are often modified. (See Grade II, 30.)

24. The following examples show correct grouping:

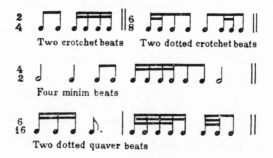

Two crotchet beats   Two dotted crotchet beats

Four minim beats

Two dotted quaver beats

RESTS

25. **Rule**: A separate rest should be used for each silent beat.

$\frac{4}{4}$ ♩ 𝄽 𝄽 ♩ ‖ not $\frac{4}{4}$ ♩ ━ ♩ ‖

$\frac{3}{4}$ ♩ 𝄽 𝄽 ‖ not $\frac{3}{4}$ ♩ ━ ‖

Exceptions:

(*a*) A semibreve rest is used for a whole bar's rest in any time except $\frac{4}{2}$, when a breve rest is used.

(*b*) In quadruple time, a half-bar's rest either at the beginning or end of the bar is shown by a single rest:

(*c*) In compound time, a one-beat rest may be shown either by a dotted rest or by two rests:

$\frac{6}{8}$ ♩ 𝄽· ‖ $\frac{6}{8}$ ♩ 𝄽 𝄾 ‖

$\frac{6}{4}$ ♩ ━· ‖ $\frac{6}{4}$ ♩ ━ 𝄽 ‖

HOW TO FIND THE KEY OF A GIVEN PIECE OF MUSIC

26. In music which is harmonized, it is usually possible to discover the key from the last chord, where the lowest note **in the bass** will usually be the key-note.

(*a*) is in A major; (*b*) is in F♯ minor.

Warning. In modern music it is not always possible to determine the key of a piece of music from the last chord, where the lowest note in the bass may not be the key-note.

27. In determining the key of a melody (without harmony and without key-signature) the following observations will be helpful:

28. If a passage contains **sharp** accidentals only, find which sharp is the last in key-signature order. The order of sharps (four for this Grade) is :

29. This last sharp is the seventh degree of the scale, and therefore the key-note will be a semitone above.

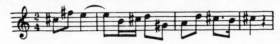

In the above tune the last sharp in order (see paragraph 28) is G♯, therefore the key-note (a semitone above) will be A. Then, according as the third degree of the scale is major or minor, so will the key be major or minor.

The key of the tune in paragraph 29 is A major.

30.

In the above tune the last sharp in order (see paragraph 28) is D♯, therefore the key-note (a semitone higher) will be E. Then, according as the third degree of the scale is major or minor, so will the key be major or minor.

The key of the tune in paragraph 30 is E minor.

31. If a passage contains **flat** accidentals only, find which flat is the last in key-signature order. The order of

flats (four for this Grade) is :

32. The last flat is the fourth degree of the scale, and therefore the key-note will be a fourth below.

33.

In the above tune the last flat in order (see paragraph 31) is E♭, therefore the key-note (a fourth below) will be B♭. Then, as the third degree of the scale is major, the key must be major.

The key of the tune in paragraph 33 is B♭ major.

34.

In the above tune the last flat in order (see paragraph 31) is A♭; but there is a flat missing—B♭ in this case. When this is so, a minor key is indicated, and the missing flat points to the seventh degree of the scale. B♮ is a semitone below C, therefore the key of the melody in paragraph 34 is C minor.

If further proof is needed, look at the third degree of the scale.

35. Some tunes contain a mixture of sharps *and* flats:

This, again, indicates a minor key, and the sharpest note—in this case F♯—is the seventh degree of the scale. The tune in paragraph 35 is therefore in G minor.

N.B. The musical student who can hear the phrase accurately will begin to feel the key centre, and will thus be able to check the scale.

BARRING AN UNBARRED PHRASE

36. In this Grade candidates will be expected to add bar-lines as well as a time-signature to a given phrase.

Points to remember:

37. The grouping of notes as described in Grade II, par. 27–29, is a safe guide.

38. In the tunes at (*a*) and (*b*) below, the actual duration of the sounds is mathematically the same in each case—quaver for quaver and semiquaver for semiquaver, etc.—but the grouping of the notes shows clearly that (*a*) is in $\frac{2}{4}$ time and (*b*) in $\frac{6}{8}$ time.

39. A phrase need not begin on the first beat of the **bar**.

40. If a rest precedes the first note, then the first bar will in itself be complete:

The grouping of the notes shows that the above tune is in simple duple time.

41. If no rest precedes the first note and the grouping shows no irregularity at the beginning or the end, then it is fairly safe to assume that the phrase begins on the first beat of the bar :

42. If, however, the grouping at the beginning and the end shows unusual features, then it can be assumed

that the phrase does *not* begin on the first beat of the
bar.

43. Furthermore, the beats which are missing at the
beginning of a phrase are made up at the end of it:

In the phrase quoted above, the detached quaver
at (*a*) and the dotted crotchet at (*b*) show unusual
groupings, and when added together they will equal
two crotchets.

The probability is, therefore, that the phrase is in
$\frac{2}{4}$ time, beginning on the last quaver of the bar :

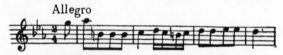

44. In the following phrase the two detached quavers at
(*a*) and the solitary one at (*c*) indicate something
unusual :

45. If the notes at (*a*) and (*c*) are added together it will
be found that they equal three quavers (♪♪♪)
or one dotted crotchet (♩.)
The phrase could therefore be in $\frac{3}{8}$ time but for the
presence of the dotted minim at (*b*).

46. This note at (*b*), together with the grouping of other
notes, shows clearly that the phrase is in ⁶⁄₈ time
(compound duple) beginning on the last two quavers
of the bar:

GRADE IV (Lower)

MAJOR SCALES OF B, F SHARP, D FLAT AND G FLAT

1. Notice how the sharps or flats are grouped in the key-signature and make sure that each new sharp or flat is placed on the correct line or space.

2. The scale of B major.
   The new sharp is A sharp. Notice that all the black notes on the keyboard are used :

   The key-signature has five sharps :

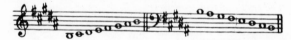

3. The scale of F sharp major.

   The new sharp is E sharp—a white note on the keyboard—and the key-signature has six sharps:

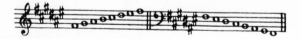

4. The scale of D flat major.
   The new flat is G flat and the key-signature has five flats. Notice that all the black notes on the keyboard are used.

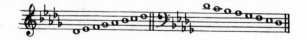

5. The scale of G flat major. The new flat is C flat—
   a white note—and the key-signature has six flats.

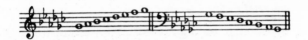

HARMONIC AND MELODIC MINOR SCALES
OF B, F SHARP, C SHARP, F AND B FLAT

6. The scale of B minor. The key-signature has **two**
   sharps (relative major D).

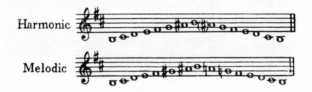

Harmonic

Melodic

7. The scale of F sharp minor.

   The key-signature has three sharps (relative major **A**).

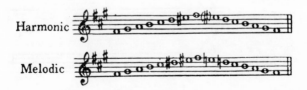

Harmonic

Melodic

8. The scale of C sharp minor.

The key-signature has four sharps (relative major E).

Harmonic

Melodic

9. The scale of F minor.

The key-signature has four flats (relative major A flat).

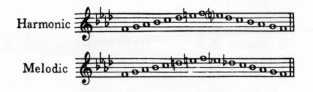

Harmonic

Melodic

10. The scale of B flat minor.

The key-signature has five flats (relative major D flat).

Harmonic

Melodic

1. Table showing Tonic Triads in close position, with root as lowest note, each with its key-signature.

INTERVALS

12. Diatonic intervals in major scales from the tonic upwards have been described in previous Grades. They are relatively the same in all major scales.
Diatonic intervals in minor scales from the tonic to the fifth have also been described and are relatively the same in all minor scales.

13. It now remains to add to these the intervals of the sixth, seventh and eighth from the tonic in the *harmonic* minor scale.

It should be specially noticed that the sixth of the harmonic minor scale forms an interval of a *minor* sixth with the tonic. It is the only new interval in this Grade.   A minor

The other two intervals are the same as in the major scales:

A minor.

Major   Perfect
7th   8th(octave)

The intervals are correspondingly the same for all minor keys.

TRANSPOSING A MELODY AT THE OCTAVE

14. To transpose a melody from treble to bass at the octave.

The melody must be re-written in the bass clef to sound one octave lower than in its present position.

HANDEL. Sonata
for 2 Oboes and Bass

Andante

Write first the bass clef, then the key-signature and time-signature. Be sure to start at the right pitch.

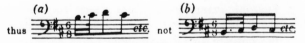

thus   (a)   not   (b)   etc.

(a) is correct, but (b) is *two* octaves below.
Put in all accidentals and see that all the intervals are correctly judged. Notice that a line in the treble becomes a space in the bass and *vice versa*.

15. To transpose a melody from bass to treble at the octave the same process applies.

Clef, key-signature, time-signature:

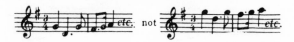

TIME

16. The various forms of Simple Time have already been described.

Compound Duple time has also been explained in Grades II and III.

The three forms of simple time, (duple, triple and quadruple), all have their compounds.

17. Compound Triple time.

There are three main beats in a bar, each consisting of a dotted note or its equivalent. The time-signatures are $\frac{9}{8}$ or $\frac{9}{4}$ or $\frac{9}{16}$.

$$\frac{9}{8} \quad \text{♩. ♩. ♩.} \qquad \frac{9}{4} \quad \text{𝅗𝅥. 𝅗𝅥. 𝅗𝅥.} \qquad \frac{9}{16} \quad \text{♪. ♪. ♪.}$$

18. Compound Quadruple time.

There are four main beats in a bar, each consisting of a dotted note or its equivalent. The time-signatures are $\frac{12}{8}$ or $\frac{12}{4}$ or $\frac{12}{16}$.

$$\frac{12}{8} \quad \text{♩. ♩. ♩. ♩.} \qquad \frac{12}{4} \quad \text{𝅗𝅥. 𝅗𝅥. 𝅗𝅥. 𝅗𝅥.} \qquad \frac{12}{16} \quad \text{♪. ♪. ♪. ♪.}$$

19. The following examples show the grouping of notes in Compound Triple and Quadruple times, which is the same in principle as the grouping in Compound Duple time:

BARRING AN UNBARRED PHRASE

20. This has been dealt with in previous grades, and all that need be added is a knowledge of the new compound times shown above.

GRADE V (Higher)

All major and all minor scales and keys with their signatures must be known in this Grade.

The only scales not included in previous Grades are:

1. (*a*) C sharp major. The new sharp is B sharp and comes as the seventh note of the scale to make the semitone between that note and the tonic (te-doh¹).

    (*b*) The key-signature has seven sharps:

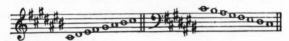

2. The scale of E flat minor. Key-signature six flats. Relative major G♭.

Harmonic

Melodic

3. The scale of G♯ minor. Key-signature five sharps. Relative major B.

Harmonic

Melodic

4. Table showing key-signatures of all Major and Minor Keys:

TECHNICAL NAMES FOR THE NOTES OF THE SCALE

5.

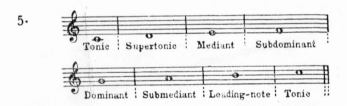

First Note.   **Tonic** is the key-note (tone-note) from which the scale takes its name.

Second Note.   **Supertonic** is the note immediately above the Tonic.

Third Note.   **Mediant** lies midway between the Tonic and the Dominant.

Fourth Note.   **Subdominant** (the lower Dominant) is so named because it is the same distance below the Tonic as the Dominant is above it—not because it is the note below the Dominant.

Fifth Note.   **Dominant** is next in importance to the Tonic, and is so called because it dominates the key.

Sixth Note.   **Submediant** (the lower Mediant) lies midway between the Tonic and the Subdominant.

Seventh Note. **Leading-note** leads up to the Tonic.

The position of the notes on the Staff in the above diagram explains the reason for some of the technical names given to the notes of the scale.

INTERVALS AND THEIR INVERSIONS FORMED ON EACH DEGREE OF THE MAJOR AND HARMONIC MINOR SCALE

6. In previous Grades diatonic intervals were formed from the key-note of the scale only. This Grade deals with intervals formed on any degree of the scale.

7. Besides the major, minor and perfect intervals already described, **augmented** and **diminished** intervals are now added.

8. A simple way of determining the nature of an interval is to find out, first of all, how many letter-names are included.

Thus, includes six letter-names (E, F,

G, A, B, C) and the interval must therefore be **a sixth of some sort.**

The student already knows from previous Grades

that ♪ is a major sixth; but in the

example under consideration the C has been raised a semitone to C♯. An interval a semitone *greater* than a major interval is said to be augmented,

therefore ♪ is an **Augmented Sixth.**

9. Similarly, in the interval ♪ three letter-

names are included (F, G, A); therefore the interval must be a third of some sort.

The student already knows from previous Grades

that ♪ is a minor third; but in the

example under consideration the A has been lowered a semitone to A♭. An interval a semitone *less* than a

minor interval is said to be diminished, ♪
therefore is a **Diminished Third.**

♪ is an **Augmented Second** and is

found between the sixth and seventh degrees of the Harmonic Minor Scale, and consists of three semitones, or one tone and one semitone.

INVERSION OF INTERVALS

10. The numerical value of an interval plus its inversion adds up to NINE.

    A 2nd when inverted becomes a 7th

3rd	,,	,,	,,	6th
4th	,,	,,	,,	5th
5th	,,	,,	,,	4th
6th	,,	,,	,,	3rd
7th	,,	,,	,,	2nd

11. All intervals, except perfect intervals, change their quality when they are inverted.

    A major interval becomes minor.

    A minor interval becomes major.

    An augmented interval becomes diminished.

    A diminished interval becomes augmented.

But a perfect interval remains perfect.

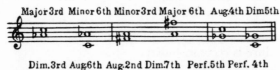

Major 3rd Minor 6th Minor 3rd Major 6th Aug.4th Dim 5th

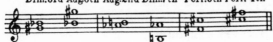

Dim.3rd Aug 6th Aug.2nd Dim.7th Perf.5th Perf. 4th

DOUBLE FLATS AND DOUBLE SHARPS

12. A double flat (♭♭) lowers the pitch of a sound two semitones.

    A double sharp (×) raises the pitch of a sound two semitones.

If the sound has already been lowered or raised a semitone, the double flat or double sharp will lower or raise the sound *one* additional semitone only.

13. When it is desired to change from a double flat to a single flat, either ♭♭ or ♭ may be used A similar method is used for a double sharp. However, the single accidental in each case is preferable.

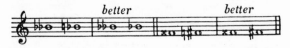

N.B. The term **Enharmonic** is used when a note changes its name but not its pitch, *e.g.* when F♯ (for convenience in notation) becomes G♭ or B♯ becomes C.

TRANSPOSING A SIMPLE MELODY INTO ANOTHER KEY

14. The transposition of a melody into another key should present little difficulty if the student possesses a reliable knowledge of intervals.

15. In tackling this type of question the following procedure is recommended:
Suppose the question to be:
Transpose this tune into F major and prefix the correct key-signature:

(a) Find the key of the tune—D major.
(b) Put the new key-signature (F major) and the time-signature on the stave:

(c) Find the position in the scale of the first few notes: 1st, 3rd, 6th degrees, etc.

(d) Then put the 1st, 3rd and 6th degrees of the new key (F major) on the stave:

(e) Find the interval between the two keys concerned (D major and F major, a minor third) and then be sure that each note of the new key (F major) is a minor third away from the original (D major).

The result will be:

16. Remember that all accidentals do not necessarily remain the same in the new key. Thus a ♯ may become a ♮, and a ♮ may become a ♭.

A tune in G minor:

when transposed to F minor would become:

SIMPLE AND COMPOUND TIMES WITH THEIR
SIGNATURES

These have been dealt with fully in previous Grades.

BARRING OF UNBARRED PHRASES

In this Grade questions may be set which require the addition of time-signatures as well as bar-lines.

17. If the phrase begins on any beat other than the first, the balance will be made up in the last bar.

18. Count the number of beats in the following tune:

The number is nine, therefore there will be three bars of triple time.
The tune begins on the last beat of the bar:

19. Eight beats could be four bars of duple time or **two** bars of quadruple time:

20. The example below could only be in $\frac{4}{4}$ time:

21. This could be in $\frac{2}{4}$ or $\frac{4}{4}$ time:

Neither of them could be in triple time.

THE COMPLETION OF INCOMPLETE BARS WITH RESTS

22. When completing bars with rests:

   (*a*) Find the value of the beat from the given time-signature:

   4 beats

   (*b*) Complete any unfinished beat:

   ⤓ = *quaver rest*

   (*c*) Add rests for any remaining beats:

   ▬ = *minim rest*

TERMS, SIGNS AND ORNAMENTS

A list of the more usual Terms and Signs has been given at the end of Grades I and II, and a more comprehensive one appears at the end of the book.

23. In Grade V Ornaments are introduced: students should be familiar with the five ornaments most commonly in use:

   1. The Turn and the inverted turn

   2. The Appoggiatura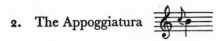

3. The Mordent and the inverted mordent

4. The Acciaccatura

5. The Trill or Shake

N.B. In the examples which follow it should be recognized that while these are acceptable and in a general way correct, there are varieties of treatment and differences of interpretation—largely dependent upon the context in which they occur and the speed at which they are required to be played.

24. (*a*) The **turn** (∽) consists of a group of four notes— the note above, the note itself, the note below, and the note itself.

(*b*) In old music the note above and below *in the scale* should be played unless otherwise indicated. In modern music an accidental is placed above or below the sign to indicate the exact note required.

(*c*) When the turn is placed between two notes it is performed thus:

(*d*) When the turn is placed after a dotted note, which equals a beat or a whole bar, the turn fills the value of the dot.

(*e*) When the dotted note is equal to a portion of a beat or a beat and a portion, a triplet is necessary: e.g.

(*f*) The inverted turn is performed in a similar way, but starting with the lower auxiliary.

25. (*a*) The **Appoggiatura** (Italian **appoggiare**, 'to lean') is not a timeless 'crushed in' note like the Acciaccatura (see paragraph 28); it is as important melodically as the note on which it 'leans,' and receives *half* the value of the principal note:

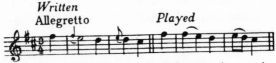

(*b*) When placed before a dotted note it receives *two-thirds* of the value of that note:

(c) When written before a chord, it is used in place
of the upper note of the chord:

26. The **Upper Mordent** (⬥) is an ornament consisting
of the principal note, the note above, and the principal note again, played as quickly as possible in the
time of the principal note:

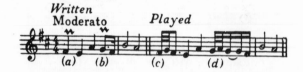

It should be noticed that the mordents at (c) and (d)
equal the exact value of the written notes at (a) and
(b). Thus (c) equals a crotchet and (d) a dotted
quaver.

27. An **Inverted Mordent** (⬥) is constructed on the
same principle, but with the lower instead of the
upper note:

An accidental placed above or below the sign indicates that the note above or below as the case may be is inflected in accordance with the accidental.

28. The **Acciaccatura** ♪ (Italian word meaning 'crushed in') is played as quickly as possible *on* the beat. It is, theoretically, timeless and is squeezed in as quickly as possible before the principal note is heard. Some pianists even play the two notes simultaneously, immediately releasing the acciaccatura and retaining the principal note.

N.B. Notice the difference between the Appoggiatura ♪ (paragraph 25) and the Acciaccatura ♪ (paragraph 28).

29. The **trill**, or **shake** (*tr* or *tr* ∿∿), is a rapid alternation of the written note and the note above it.

    (*a*) In modern music the trill usually begins on the written note itself, and ends with a small turn below the written note, which necessitates the insertion of a triplet immediately before that turn. The turn is usually indicated in semiquavers, but is played in whatever value of notes has been used in the trill

(*b*) In earlier music (up to and including Haydn and Mozart) it is generally intended that the trill should begin on the upper of the two notes, which means that there will be an even number of notes and no triplet.

(*c*) When the trill occurs on a repeated note it will always begin with the upper note.

TONIC TRIADS IN CLOSE POSITION
AND THEIR INVERSIONS IN MAJOR AND MINOR KEYS

Tonic triads in root position and in close position have already been dealt with in previous grades.

30. The only new keys in this grade are:

(1) C♯ major

(2) E♭ minor

(3) G♯ minor

It is now required that the inversions of major and minor triads should be known.

31. A triad in root position consists of the root, its third and its fifth.

And it may be as well here to define the word *Root*, for some confusion exists as to its use.

The Root is the note from which a chord originates. In the following examples (1) is the tonic chord of A♭ major with the root of the chord at the top. (2) is the subdominant chord of A♭ major (Root D♭) with the tonic of the *scale* at the top. In both cases, however, the top note is A♭.

32. **A first inversion** of a tonic triad in close position has the third in the bass, the fifth in the middle and the root at the top :

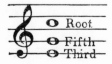

It is often called a chord of the $\frac{6}{3}$ because the notes in it—from the bass upwards—are respectively a third and a sixth from the bass. Further abbreviated, it is known as the Chord of the Sixth.

33. **A second inversion** of a tonic triad in close position has the fifth in the bass, the root in the middle and the third at the top :

It is often called a chord of the $\frac{6}{4}$, because the notes in it—from the bass upwards—are respectively a fourth and a sixth from the bass.

Tonic triads and their inversions are formed in precisely the same way in all other major and minor keys.

PRIMARY CHORDS

The three Primary Chords (I, IV and V) in root position in any key (root, third or fifth at the top, with three notes on the treble staff and one on the bass).

34. This involves the writing of chords in four parts and is, in itself, an introduction to the study of harmony.

Since there are only three notes in a triad, it is now left to the student—when writing in four parts—to decide (*a*) which note should be doubled; (*b*) how to arrange the chord on the two staves.

35. For present purposes the best note to double is the root.

36. The syllabus requires that three notes shall be placed

on the treble staff and one on the bass, and this usually determines a satisfactory arrangement of the remaining notes.

The student is further helped when the question states (as it generally does) which note is to be placed at the top.

37. Suppose the question to be: ' Write the dominant chord of E major in four parts (three notes in the treble and one in the bass) with the third of the chord (or the leading note of the scale) at the top.'

The dominant chord of E major has B as its root and F♯ and D♯ as the remaining notes.

38. In dealing with the above type of question the following plan will be found helpful; it holds good for all major and minor keys:

(a) Put B on the bass staff.

(b) Put the third (D♯) at the top.

(c) Add the two notes of the chord (B and F♯) which come immediately below the top note

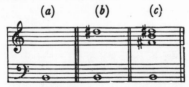

39. If it is not specified which note of the chord is to be at the top, it is advisable to have the gap between the bass and the note immediately above it:

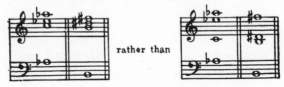

rather than

WRITING A RHYTHM (ON ONE NOTE)
TO FIT GIVEN WORDS

40. The procedure has already been described in Grade
II, 30–31.

41. Further instances of faulty accentuation are quoted
below, and the student may be asked to state his
reasons for the rejection of the one and the retention
of the other:

The objections to (a) are obvious. Although the
phrase is in the normal length of four bars, the
accents fall in the wrong places and the result is
clumsy and unmusical.

42.

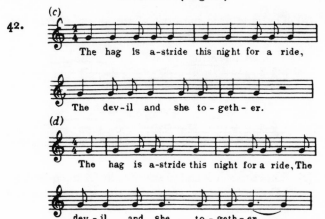

(c)

The hag is a-stride this night for a ride,

The dev-il and she to-geth-er.

(d)

The hag is a-stride this night for a ride, The

dev-il and she to-geth-er. ___

Similar objections apply to (c) as opposed to the more natural rhythm of (d).

ADDING AN ANSWERING PHRASE TO A GIVEN PHRASE

The answering phrase should be of the same **length** as the given phrase.

43. The following hints will help the student to make the answering phrase both logical and musical:

(a) The given phrase usually modulates, that is, changes key, to the dominant ; let the answering phrase lead back to the tonic :

Andante

Answering phrase

(b) The rhythmic patterns of the given phrase can well be used in the answering phrase:

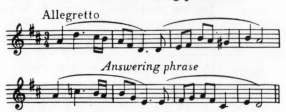

(c) Sometimes it is stated specifically in the question: ' Do not simply copy the time-pattern of the given part.'

In this case set up a new rhythmic-pattern and try to use some of its material in different ways—develop it, to use the technical word.

(d) Some contrary motion in the answering phrase often adds strength and new interest to the original:

GRADE VI (Intermediate)

All scales with their key-signatures should now be familiar. In this Grade both forms of the minor scale, harmonic and melodic, must be known, no choice being left to the candidate. Reference can be made to Grade II, in which the construction of the minor scale in both forms is explained in detail.

THE HARMONIC CHROMATIC SCALE

1. The word chromatic means colourful. A chromatic scale is one in which all the steps are semitones.

   The harmonic chromatic scale is so written that each note can be harmonized in relation to the tonic of the scale. For instance, if C is the tonic then every note of the scale can be harmonized in relation to the key of C.

   To write the scale take first all the notes of the scale of C major.

   Add to these the notes of the scale of C minor (in both forms) which are not found in the major scale.

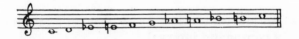

Only two notes have now to be added to complete the run of semitones.

The first note is between C and D; the second note is between F and G.

Is the first to be C sharp or D flat? Is the second to be F sharp or G flat?

The answers are : D flat, the diatonic semitone above C, the tonic ; and, F sharp, the diatonic semitone below G, the dominant, because these notes are needed in the formation of some of the more elaborate chords in the key.

Here is the complete scale:

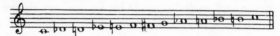

2. Notice that the tonic and dominant are the only two notes whose letter names are used once. The same process applies to all keys.

INTERVALS

3. When the two notes forming a semitone have different letter names, the semitone is **diatonic.**

When the two notes forming a semitone have the same letter name the semitone is **chromatic.**

diatonic   chromatic
semitone   semitone

Remember that this only applies to semitones.

4. An interval which is greater than an octave is called a **compound interval.**

major ninth   major   minor   perfect
               tenth   eleventh twelfth

These have the same designation (major, minor, etc.) as their corresponding simple intervals of a second, third, or fourth, etc.

TRIADS

5. Each note of a major or minor scale has its own triad of which it forms the root.

In the key of C major the triads are as follows:

Tonic Super- Mediant Sub- Dominant Sub- Leading
       tonic   dominant   mediant note

There are three major triads: Tonic, Subdominant and Dominant.
There are three minor triads: Supertonic, Mediant and Submediant.
There is one diminished triad: on the Leading note. It is called a diminished triad because the fifth is diminished and not perfect.

6. Key of A minor:

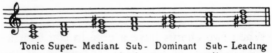

Tonic Super- Mediant Sub- Dominant Sub- Leading
       tonic   dominant   mediant note

In a minor key there are two minor triads: Tonic and Subdominant.
There are two major triads: Dominant and Submediant.
There are two diminished triads: Supertonic and Leading note.
There is one augmented triad: the Mediant. This triad is called augmented because the fifth (C to G sharp) is an augmented fifth.
All these triads can be inverted, but in practice the second inversions of several of them are of little value.

THE THREE PRIMARY CHORDS

7. These chords must now be written so as to follow
each other in smooth harmonic progressions. The
spacing of notes is the same as in Grade V.

Avoid unnecessary jumps:

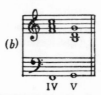

When two chords have a note in common keep that
note in the same part, moving each other part to the
note nearest to it in the next chord.

Here C is kept in the top part of the first two chords
while G remains the second note from the top in the
last three chords.

The leading note should rise to the tonic.

(d)

V   I   V   I
good   bad

Move by step where possible, but avoid similar motion in all the parts at once.

(e)

IV   I   V   I

Compare this with the example (c). The chords are the same but notes in common have not remained in the same part and the leading note has been allowed to fall.

No two parts may move together in octaves or fifths—consecutive octaves or fifths, as they are called.

HARMONIC RHYTHM

8. Rhythm in music is influenced by the position in the bar which is assigned to each chord. A change of harmony on a strong beat gives emphasis to the beat,

but the same chord from a weak beat to a strong beat does not give the necessary feeling of accent. The placing of chords in a progression is therefore a matter of vital importance to the rhythm and shape of the music.

In the above example the music seems to stick at the fourth and fifth chords marked ×.

It is best to avoid using the same bass note from a weak beat to a strong beat.

When the two chords from a weak beat to a strong beat have no note in common, the effect is that of a strong accent.

There are, however, cases where an accent is felt on the strong beat even without a change of harmony. A leap can create an accent: the greater the leap the greater the stress:

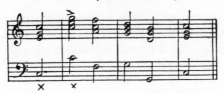

The same two chords can be used from weak to strong beat at the start of a piece or new section of a piece :

or when the harmony has lasted throughout the whole preceding bar :

Notice that the music is never ' stationary.' It is the movement which creates the accent.

CADENCES

9. Music, like language, has its punctuation, its full stops, its semicolons and its commas. These stops are indicated by chords specially selected and arranged to give a logical end to a musical phrase or sentence. These phrase-endings are called Cadences.

10. At the end of a piece a Cadence is generally chosen
which gives the greatest sense of finality. The two
simplest chord formations which give this effect are
(a) The Dominant chord (V) followed by the Tonic
chord (I). (b) The Subdominant chord (IV) followed
by the Tonic (I).

(a) V to I are used to form what is known as a
Perfect Cadence (or Full Close).

V I
C major

V I
A minor

(b) IV to I are used to form what is known as a
Plagal Cadence.

IV I
C major

IV I
A minor

Both Perfect and Plagal Cadences end on the Tonic
chord (I). For present purposes these may be com-
pared with full stops, giving, as they do, the feeling
of finality to a musical phrase.

11. Where stops other than full stops are required,
chords are selected which, though pointing to the
end of the phrase, suggest that there is more to
follow. The two simplest of the many chord formations which give this effect are:

(*a*) The Tonic chord (I) following by the Dominant chord (V).

(*b*) The Subdominant chord (IV) followed by the Dominant (V).

These chords, when they occur at cadence points in this order, give two forms of what is known as an **Imperfect Cadence** (or Half Close).

(*a*) I to V.

I   V   I   V
C major   A minor

Notice that this is merely a Perfect Cadence in reverse.

(*b*) IV to V.

IV V   IV V
C major   A minor

When the bass moves by step (IV to V) there is a danger of consecutive fifths and octaves. These can be avoided by the use of contrary motion between the bass and the other parts.

12. A knowledge of the three Primary Chords in all major and minor keys and the Cadences formed by

them will enable the candidate to answer such questions as the following:
'Complete the harmonies and name the Cadence formed by the last two chords.'

First the key: B minor.
Then, what are the chords? I, IV and V.
The Cadence is therefore Imperfect (IV to V).
Now fill in the notes of the harmony, remembering the sharpened leading-note which is the third of the Dominant chord in a minor key.

WRITING A MELODY TO GIVEN WORDS

13. The rhythmic side of this question, which has already been dealt with, is half the battle.

The melody will probably have to contain two four-bar phrases and will be about eight bars in length.

First write the rhythm:

>   >   >
Ben Battle was a soldier bold,

>   >   >
And used to war's alarms;

>   >   >
But a cannon-ball took off his legs,

>   >   >
So he laid down his arms.   Hood.

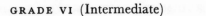

Ben Battle was a soldier bold and used to wars a-

larms   But a cannon-ball took off his legs so

He laid down his arms

Now notes must be chosen to suit the mood of the words. The music must be martial in character. Key B flat major:

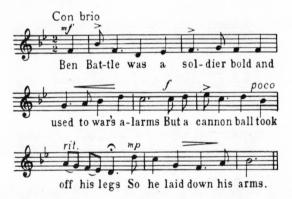

Expression marks should always be added.

As the rhythm of the melody is suggested by the accents of the words, so must the style of the melody be governed by the mood of the words, and its shape by their sense and meaning.

As the words are punctuated by commas and stops, so the music must have its phrases and its cadences. A cadence should be implied at the end of the first phrase, generally an Imperfect Cadence.

14. Sometimes words give scope for a great variety of imaginative treatment:

> *The twilight is sad and cloudy,*
> *The wind blows wild and free,*
> *And like the wings of sea birds*
> *Flash the white caps of the sea.*

LONGFELLOW.

The first line will be quiet and subdued. The second line can suggest a gust of wind. The third line can build up to a climax on the word 'flash.' These words seem to demand a minor key.

15. A more exciting effect at the end can be obtained by shifting the accents forward from strong to weak beats, using what is known as syncopation.

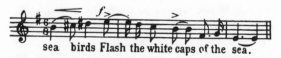

This device can give even greater emphasis to a word than if it fell on an ordinary accented beat. Syncopation should be used sparingly.

ADDING AN ANSWERING PHRASE TO COMPLETE A GIVEN FOUR-BAR PHRASE

16. There are two things to aim at:
    (1) To add a phrase of four bars which by its character will balance the given phrase.
    (2) To make the whole musical sentence sound a complete and continuous progression of eight bars.

RHYTHM

17. It is not sufficient merely to reproduce the rhythm of the given phrase, but neither is it desirable to invent entirely new rhythm. There should be some connection between the rhythmic pattern of the two sections.

The given phrase will contain several rhythmic patterns, which in some cases overlap.

(1) ♩. ♫ ♩ (2) ♩. ♫ (3) ♫ ♫ (4) ♫ ♩ (5) ♫ ♩

The answering phrase can contain any or all of these in a different order:

It keeps the family likeness but assumes its own personality.

The repetition of the triplet figure gives a cumulative effect as well as the suggestion of a sequence.

The restatement of the opening rhythm coming at the end gives a feeling of balance as well as finality.

PITCH

18. The actual notes are, of course, a matter of personal taste, and any notes will be accepted as long as the sentence finishes in the right key and is not devoid of melodic shape.

   There should be some sort of climax about halfway through the answering phrase.

   The given phrase may contain some characteristic interval or series of intervals which should have their complement in the answering phrase.

   In the above example the jump of a seventh in the second bar has a significance which must not be ignored.

   It is sometimes useful to invert the shape of part of the given phrase:

Here is a possible answer to the above example:

GRADE VII (Advanced)

Major, minor and harmonic chromatic scales in all keys have been dealt with in previous Grades.

Students are now expected to be able to find the **major** and **minor** scales in which a given interval occurs.

1. To find the keys in which a given interval may occur diatonically (*i.e.* when both notes belong to a diatonic scale in whatever key is being considered), first find the number and quality of the given interval.

2. Take the following question:

   ' In how many keys can the interval be found? '

   (*a*) Find the number and quality of the interval given. It is a major third.

   (*b*) Find on which degrees of the major and minor scales a major third can occur.

Major scale

1 2 3 4 5 6 7 8

In a major scale a major third occurs between:

therefore the two notes
of the given interval
will be the:

1st and 3rd notes of the scale of B♭ major.
4th and 6th   „   „   „   F major.
5th and 7th   „   „   „   E♭ major.

Now take the harmonic minor scale in the same
way:

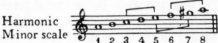

(c) In a harmonic minor scale a major third occurs
between:

3–5,   5–7 and 6–8

therefore the two notes of the given interval

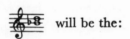 will be the:

3rd and 5th notes of the scale of G minor.
5th and 7th   „   „   „   E♭ minor.
6th and 8th   „   „   „   D minor.

3. One more example should make the process clear:

'In how many keys can the interval
be found?'

(a) It is a Diminished Fifth.

(b) In a major scale:

A **Diminished Fifth** occurs between 7–4; therefore the two notes of the given interval will be the:

7th and 4th notes of the scale of E major.

(c) Now take the harmonic minor scale in the same way:

1 2 3 4 5 6 7 8=1 2 3 4 5 6 7 8

In a harmonic minor scale a Diminished Fifth occurs between 2–6, 7–4.

Therefore the two notes of the given interval will be the:

2nd and 6th notes of the scale of C♯ minor.

7th and 4th   ,,   ,,   ,,   E minor.

TERMS, SIGNS AND ABBREVIATIONS

In addition to those mentioned in previous Grades, the following signs and abbreviations should also be known:

4. Repetitions of the same note are shown thus:

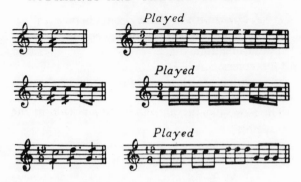

5. When two notes are to be repeated alternately the following abbreviation is used:

6. The repetition of whole groups or bars :—

7. 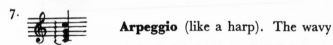 **Arpeggio** (like a harp). The wavy

line indicates, in keyboard music, that the chord should be broken or spread, usually upwards. If the spread is intended to be downwards (now seldom used)

it is written: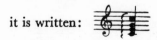

COMMON CHORDS ON I, IV, V, VI

Common Chords on the Tonic, Subdominant, Dominant and Submediant (I, IV, V, VI) laid out as for four voices S.A.T.B., two notes on the Treble Staff and two on the Bass, and also in succession as in the four cadences.

8. The four voices have now to be written two on each stave and it is important that they should be spaced correctly. Adjacent parts should not be more than an octave apart, except the lowest two:

9. To save time in writing, chords may be described by Roman numerals, thus:

I	=	Tonic, root position.
V	=	Dominant, root position.
IVb	=	Subdominant, first inversion.
Ic	=	Tonic, second inversion.
Etc.		

10. The **Interrupted Cadence** (V–VI) is the only new cadence introduced in this Grade. If the music seems to be leading to a perfect cadence but, when it should arrive, the Dominant chord (V) is followed by some chord other than the tonic—usually the Submediant (VI)—the cadence is called an ' Interrupted Cadence.'

There are other forms of the Interrupted Cadence in which V can be followed by almost any other chord (see (*b*) above), but for present purposes the above example at (*a*) (V–VI) will suffice.

11. Care must be taken in the writing of parts, since the two chords (V and VI) are on adjacent degrees of the scale, that consecutive fifths and octaves do not appear as in the following example:

12. (*a*) The major third of the Dominant chord (V) is the leading-note and, as such, should rise to the Tonic (I).

(*b*) The octave G and the fifth D in the Dominant chord (V) should both move downwards. In this way all danger of consecutive fifths and octaves is removed:

It will be noticed at * above that the third of the chord has been doubled. It is not only permissible but necessary when V is followed by VI; but it is not recommended in other progressions.

HARMONIZATION IN FOUR PARTS OF A SIMPLE MELODY
OR OF AN UNFIGURED BASS

A knowledge of chords I, II, IV, V, VI and their inversions is expected in this Grade.

13. The only new chord here is the Supertonic (II) and this may also be used in an Imperfect Cadence (II–V).

N.B. The Supertonic chord (II) in a minor key, being a diminished triad, is best used only in first inversion.

14. Other chords can precede the Dominant in an Imperfect Cadence. Examples are given below:

15. The $^6_4$ $^5_3$ approach to a Perfect Cadence is often encountered and should be known :

A $\frac{6}{4}$ chord used in this way is called a ' Cadential $\frac{6}{4}$.'

16. The second inversion of the triad ($\frac{6}{4}$) is best avoided, except when it occurs in the cadence $\frac{6}{4}\frac{5}{3}$ as shown in paragraph 15; but it can be used with good effect when it is approached and quitted by step in the lowest part as in the following example :

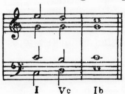

In this case it is called a ' Passing $\frac{6}{4}$.'

UNACCENTED PASSING-NOTES

17. Passing-notes are notes which do not belong to the chord and are therefore unessential to the harmony. They are discords and as such must, at any rate for the present, be approached and quitted by step.

18. They may lead to a note of the same chord :

or to a note of another chord:

In the above examples, passing-notes are marked ×.

THE CONSTRUCTION OF A PHRASE
ON A GIVEN HARMONIC BASIS

19. The only original work involved here is the placing of the chords and the shape of the melody.

The latter is often enhanced by the judicious use of unaccented passing-notes.

They are marked × in the following example:

WRITING A MELODY TO GIVEN WORDS

The procedure has been shown in Grade VI.

COMPLETING A MELODY OF WHICH THE BEGINNING IS GIVEN (THE WHOLE MELODY LIMITED TO 12 BARS)

Simple modulations may be required, *e.g.* to the Dominant, the Subdominant, the Relative major or minor.

20. It should be borne in mind that the modulation has
to be made by the melody only, since no accompany-
ing harmony is asked for. When modulating, therefore, it is important to employ such notes as will
establish firmly the new key.

21. In the following examples (where we will suppose that
a modulation to the Dominant has been asked for),
that at (a) might well be in C major throughout;
but in the example at (b) the presence of the F♯
indicates that a modulation has, in fact, taken place.

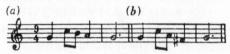

22. The following question is taken from a paper set by
the Associated Board of the Royal Schools of Music
(Grade VII) in March 1955:
'Complete the following melody (the whole melody
limited to 12 bars). Pass through the keys of C
minor, B♭ major and end in G minor. Add suitable
markings.'

23. The following is a possible working of the question.
At (a) a clear modulation to C minor is indicated
by the A♭ and B♮, while at (b) a modulation to B♭
major—in spite of the absence of any accidentals—
may safely be assumed. A return to G minor at (c)
is firmly established by the presence of the F♯ and
B♭ in the penultimate bar.

ADDING ANOTHER MELODY
ABOVE OR BELOW A GIVEN MELODY

24. The student who is able to harmonize a melody or add three parts above an unfigured bass should find no undue difficulty in adding one melody above or below another.

25. It is advisable to think harmonically, for if the melody can be supplied with harmonies mentally and the modulations 'spotted,' many difficult places will be made plain.

The following observations will be found helpful.

26. The intervals most frequently used will be the third and the sixth:

27. Contrary motion often produces a stronger effect than similar motion.

28. The fifth is best avoided because of its bare sound, but when used as at × below, where the *upper* part moves by step, it is always satisfactory:

29. The fourth can be used when the *lower* part moves by step:

or when it is treated as a Passing-note:

30. The second and seventh, being dissonant, are best treated as Passing-notes:

ANALYSIS OF THE RHYTHMIC STRUCTURE OF A MELODY, AND PHRASING

31. In this Grade students should be able to phrase a melody and to comment on the length and balance of phrases.

   Points to remember:

32. The normal lengths of phrases are two or four bars, though phrases of other lengths can also be found.

33. Look for the Cadences, for a new phrase may begin immediately afterwards.

   Cadences can often be 'spotted' by a long note in the melody:

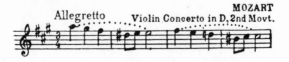

34. On the other hand the melody may move while the
bass has the long note:

35. Look for Sequences; they usually show the beginning
and end of a phrase:

36. The term 'Sequence' is applied to the repetition of
a melody (with or without its harmony) at another
level, higher or lower. If the repetition is only in
the melody (the harmony being varied) it is called a
Melodic Sequence; if in the harmony also, a Harmonic Sequence.

37. If the opening notes of a tune are repeated, this
may well be the recapitulation and the beginning
of another phrase.

38. Suppose this to be the question:
   (1) Add phrase marks to show the rhythmic structure
       of this tune.
   (2) In which bars is there an example of sequence?
   (3) To what key does the tune modulate in bar 6
       and in the first half of bar 7?
   (4) Comment on the balance and length of phrases.

---

* This sign ♯ is called a 'Direct' and is used at the end of a
line or page to give warning of the next note.

BACH
St. Matthew Passion

39. A sequence occurs in bar 4; (a) is answered a third lower by (b).

A longer sequence is in bars 5–7 where (c) is answered by (d).

40. The key is C minor.

A modulation to B♭ major occurs in bar 6, and to A♭ major in the first half of bar 7. Although there is a D♮ in the second beat of bar 7, the student who can harmonize the passage mentally would not be far wrong in arriving at a chord of A♭ major on the third beat.

Bach's actual harmonies
are:

Modulations to other keys are certainly possible here, but they involve more knowledge of harmony than is expected of the student in this Grade.

BALANCE OF PHRASES. PHRASE LENGTHS

41. The opening phrase ending on the note G in bar 3 is answered by one of similar length ending on the note G in bar 5.

42. In bars 5 and 6 the phrase at (c) is answered by the sequential one at (d).

43. Several short phrases which balance each other occur in bars 7-10; they are rounded off by the final one beginning on B♮ in bar 10.

SIMPLE HARMONIC ANALYSIS

Points to remember:

44. (a) Find out the key of the passage—whether major or minor.

(b) Find which note of the scale is the **Root** of the chord—Tonic, Dominant, Supertonic, etc.

(c) And thus determine the position of the chord—whether root position, first inversion or second inversion.

N.B. To save time in writing students are strongly advised to use the convenient formula described in paragraph 9.

45. Describe the numbered chords in the following passage and name the Cadences at (a) and (b). Explain the notes marked ×.

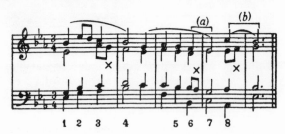

46. Specimen Answer:

Key E♮ major.

1. Tonic triad, root position   .   .   .   I
2. Tonic triad, first inversion   .   .   .   Ib
3. Subdominant triad, root position   .   .   IV
4. Dominant triad, root position   .   .   V
5. Tonic triad, second inversion   .   .   Ic
6. Dominant triad, root position   .   .   V
7. Submediant triad, root position   .   .   VI
8. Subdominant triad, root position   .   .   IV

Notes marked × are Passing-notes, correctly approached and quitted by step.

Cadence at (a) Interrupted cadence.

Cadence at (b) Plagal cadence.

47. Describe each chord in the following passage, name the Cadences at (a) and (b) and explain the notes marked ×.

48. **Specimen Answer:**

Key B minor.

1. Supertonic triad, first inversion . . IIb
2. Dominant triad, root position . . V
3. Dominant triad, first inversion . . Vb
4. Tonic triad, root position . . . I
5. Tonic triad, first inversion . . . Ib
6. Subdominant triad, root position . IV
7. Dominant triad, root position . . V
8. Submediant triad, root position . . VI
9. Subdominant triad, root position . IV
10. Tonic triad, second inversion . . Ic
11. Dominant triad, root position . . V
12. Tonic triad, root position . . . I

Notes marked × are Passing-notes, correctly approached and quitted by step.

Cadence at (a) Interrupted cadence.

Cadence at (b) Perfect cadence.

GRADE VIII (Final)

CLEFS

1. In addition to treble and bass clefs (G and F) there are two other clefs in regular use. These are C clefs for which the following signs are used:

The line on which the sign is centred is middle C.
The Alto clef is sometimes used for the Alto voice in choral writing and generally for the viola in instrumental writing. Notice the position of sharps and flats.

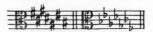

Notice that middle C is on the middle line.
The Tenor clef was used in old music for the Tenor voice in choral writing, and is still used in instrumental writing for the Tenor Trombone and often for the upper notes of the 'cello and Bassoon.
Middle C is on the fourth line. Notice the position of the sharps and flats.

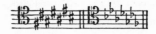

The following fragment of a Bach Chorale is set out first in short score, then in open score with C clefs for Alto and Tenor.

FOUR-PART CHORDS WITH THEIR INVERSIONS
FORMED ON ALL DEGREES OF THE MAJOR
AND MINOR SCALE

Three new chords have to be learnt in this Grade:
(1) the triad on the mediant of the scale; (2) the triad
on the leading-note; (3) the chord of the dominant
seventh.

The Mediant Chord

2. The triad on the mediant (III) is a chord which
   needs careful use. Its character depends on the fact
   that it has two notes (its root and third) in common
   with the tonic chord, and two notes (its third and
   fifth) in common with the dominant chord. It can

well be introduced in the course of a phrase to help
delay the approach to a cadence.

The leading-note of the scale seems to lose something
of its character when it becomes the fifth of the
mediant chord. It *falls* quite naturally in the progressions III to VI and III to IV:

In using the mediant chord care must be taken to
place it with due reference to the harmonic rhythm
of the phrase (see VI, 8).

The following are some of its uses:

Notice the chords which precede and follow III.

3. The mediant chord in a **Minor** key contains the
discord of an augmented fifth. The leading note,
being the discordant note, must appear in the same
part in the preceding chord and must rise to the tonic.

The Chord on the Leading Note

4. The triad on the leading note has both strength and usefulness. It is generally to be found in its first inversion (VIIb).

   The root, being the leading note, must never be doubled, but either the fifth or the third may be doubled with good effect.

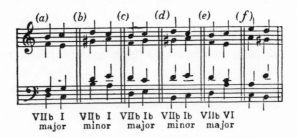

| VIIb I | VIIb I | VIIb Ib | VIIb Ib | VIIb VI |
| major | minor | major | minor | major |

VIIb to I is another form of the perfect cadence.

At (e) VIIb is followed by VI. This is only possible in a major key.

In a minor key the supertonic, II, is also a diminished triad and is treated in the same way as VII in the major key (see VII, 13).

The Chord of the Dominant Seventh

5. The chord of the dominant seventh is V with the addition of the minor seventh from the root:

Its use is not hard to grasp if it is considered as a decoration of the dominant chord.

It has its origin in a passing note (a) which, by familiar use, became a harmony note (b) in its own right.

As a general rule the seventh must fall to the note below it, allowing the leading note to rise:

In exceptional cases the seventh may remain as a note common to the next chord in which case the following chord will be an inversion of (IV).

There are three inversions:

1st Inversion   2nd Inversion   3rd Inversion

6. The second inversion can also accept another resolution in which the seventh rises : i.e. when the second inversion is followed by first inversion of Tonic.

Modulation to Related Keys

7. The related keys are:

   Tonic, Dominant and Subdominant with their relative minors or majors as the case may be.

   It will be seen that every note of a major scale except the leading note can be regarded as the Tonic of a related key.

   In a minor key the supertonic is excluded and the flattened sixth and seventh are related tonics.

   Thus, in C major the Subdominant (F) has D minor as its relative.

   In A minor the Subdominant (D) has F major (the flattened sixth) as its relative.

   The Dominant of A minor (E) has G major (the flattened seventh) as its relative.

8. It is possible, by means of modulation, to pass smoothly from one key to any other of its related keys. Modulation always requires an accidental.

If the new key has more sharps in its signature, its leading note will have to be sharpened.

If there are more flats in the new key its dominant seventh will have to be flattened (4th of new scale).

The following examples show what accidentals need to be used when modulating from C major to its related keys:

Four chords at least are necessary. The second is the pivot chord which belongs to the first key and approaches the dominant of the new key.

The accidental is not necessarily in the treble part. A most unpromising melody containing no accidentals often gives great scope for modulation.

The above examples give only the bare necessities. It is desirable to know not only *how* to modulate but *when* to modulate. Too many modulations make the music sound restless, and too few may make it sound dull and uneventful. The key of the piece should be firmly established before any excursions are made to its relations. The examples assume that this has been done.

Passing Notes

9. The use of unaccented passing notes has already been shown in Grade VII.

   A passing note may occur on an accent with strong effect, becoming what is known as an Accented Passing Note. In its simplest form it must be approached and quitted by step from one essential harmony note to another.

   An accented passing note only sounds well if the note on which it resolves is not already sounding in another part.

Figured Bass

10. Figures written under a bass part indicate the chords which are to be used. Figured bass is a time-honoured form of musical shorthand.

   The figures show the intervals from the bass which are to be used. Thus $\frac{5}{3}$ is an ordinary triad; $\frac{6}{3}$ is a first inversion; $\frac{6}{4}$ is a second inversion.

   These figures are reduced to a minimum in practice, for $\frac{5}{3}$ is always understood when there are no figures under a note, and $\frac{6}{3}$ is understood by a plain 6. A sharp, flat, or natural under a note refers to the third from the bass.

   The dominant seventh in root position is written as a plain 7. Its inversions are $\frac{6}{5}$, $\frac{4}{3}$ and $\frac{4}{2}$. With a $\frac{6}{5}$ the third is understood. With $\frac{4}{3}$ and $\frac{4}{2}$ the sixth is understood.

A line means that the note (or notes) of the preceding figure must be held.

The notes can be arranged in any order.

Two-part Writing

11. The adding of another melody above or below a given melody has already been done in Grade VII. In this Grade, however, dominant sevenths, modulations and accented passing notes may be freely implied.

Simple Pianoforte Style

12. The pianoforte has a very wide range of tone and expression, and its compass extends far beyond that of the human voice. For present purposes, however, a simple style of writing is required and the student is not expected to have all the resources of the instrument at his command.

It is not necessary to keep to four-part harmony, but the notes should be arranged and spaced for the convenience of the hands and fingers.

The pianoforte has limited sustaining power. To compensate for this it is often desirable to supply rhythmic figures or a moving accompaniment. These may consist of broken chord or arpeggio figures and can include passing notes. Rests can often be used with good effect.

The use of the sustaining pedal should be understood. This can give continuity to the harmonic progressions, no matter how fragmentary they may appear.

'Complete the following in simple pianoforte style—quaver movement should be fairly constant in the left hand.'

The first bar and melody only are given.

First decide what harmonies are suitable. The harmonic 'skeleton' may be sketched in before any quavers are written:

Then the given figure (the first bar) can be developed by ' decorating ' the harmony with quaver movement.

In spite of the apparent liberties which may be taken in pianoforte writing, all the principles of good harmonic progression and part-writing must be just as carefully considered in writing for key-board as for voices, although the actual application of these principles will naturally differ.

Writing a Melody to Given Words

13. This is the same as in previous Grades except that the use of modulation gives additional scope.

Completing a Melody of which the Beginning is Given

14. The melody will be longer than hitherto. A knowledge of form and structure is expected. Modulations will be necessary to give length and variety to the melody

   Not only must phrases be marked, but they must be clearly punctuated by implied cadences.

   Use can be made of sequences and the rhythmic figures suggested in the opening phrase should be fully exploited.

   The final phrase may well contain a reference to the opening.

Analysis of the Rhythmic Structure of a Melody and Phrasing

15. Some of the greatest melodies are found to be quite unconventional when their rhythmic structure is analysed.

   The famous Air from the Suite in D by Bach is a case in point:

The long note at the start looks incongruous, but it will be seen that it is balanced by a long note at the beginning of each phrase. These long notes become shorter and the short notes more numerous as the melody proceeds. It is cumulative in effect.

The first phrase (a) is two bars in length and modulates to the dominant.

The second phrase (b) with only a minim at the start is one bar in length and modulates to the supertonic. There is overlapping between (b) and the third phrase (c) which forms a sequence with (b) and modulates back to the tonic.

The last phrase (d) bears some resemblance to the first phrase but is an elaborate variation of it, modulating again to the dominant.

The final note of one phrase can often coincide with the first note of its successor, as at (c) and (d). This device of overlapping gives continuity to a melody

Analysis of Harmonic Progression

16. This requires the ability to name cadences:

    To describe all common chords with their inversions:

    To recognise the dominant seventh with its inversions:

    To name modulations.

    All this should be possible if the candidate has a working knowledge of what has gone before.

GENERAL TERMS

It is obviously impossible to make a list of signs and terms which will correspond accurately with the requirements of each Grade.

The more usual signs and terms to be found in Grades I and II have been listed separately, but hereafter a more comprehensive alphabetical list has been compiled, even at the risk of duplicating the information previously given.

Any good musical dictionary will supply those items which are not included here.

A	At, to, by
A Cappella . .	(*lit.* in the church style.) Unaccompanied vocal music
Accelerando ⎫ Accel. ⎭ . .	Gradually faster
Ad libitum ⎫ . . Ad lib. ⎭	At pleasure. The speed and manner of performance are left to the performer
Acciaccatura . .	See Grade V, 28
Adagio . . .	Slow
Adagietto . .	Rather slow
Adagissimo . .	Very slow
Affrettando . .	Hurrying, pressing onwards
Agitato . . .	Agitated
Alla Breve . .	Formerly stood for four minims in a bar, now more often indicates two minim beats.

Allargando	. .	Getting slower, with an implication also of generally bigger tone.
Allegro .	. .	Lively, fast
Allegretto	. .	Rather lively (but less so than Allegro)
Andante	. .	(*lit.* walking). At a moderate pace
Andantino	. .	Alternatively faster or slower than Andante.
Anima .	. .	Soul. Con anima, with deep feeling
Animato	. .	Animated
A piacere	. .	At pleasure
Appassionato .	.	Passionately
Appoggiatura .	.	A grace-note. See V, 25
Arco	. .	A direction to string players to resume the use of the bow after a passage of pizzicato
Arpeggio	. .	See Grade VII, 7
Assai .	. .	Very
A tempo	. .	In time, i.e. resuming normal speed after a deviation
Attacca .	. .	Go on at once
B (*Ger.*) .	. .	The note B flat. H is used for B natural. Hence:
Bémol (*Fr.*) Bemolle	. .	The Flat sign (♭)
Ben, Bene	. .	Well
Bewegt (*Ger.*) .	.	With movement
Bis (*Lat.*)	. .	Twice
Breit (*Ger.*)	. .	Broad
Bravura (con.)	.	(With) boldness and spirit

Breve	. . .	(*lit.* short). Originally a note of relatively short duration, but now the longest note, equal to four minims
Brillante	. .	Brilliant
Brio	. .	Vigour
Calando	.	Decreasing both tone and speed
Cantabile ⎱ Cantando ⎰	. .	In a singing style
Cantilena	.	Short, song-like piece
Capo	. .	(*lit.* head). The beginning (**da** capo—from the beginning)
Capriccio		A caprice (a piece in free-light-hearted style)
Coda	. .	(*lit.* a tail.) A passage added at the end of a movement to make a satisfactory finish
Col, coll', ⎱ colla, collo ⎰	. .	With the
Col legno	.	A direction to string players to use the wood of the bow
Colla parte	.	(*lit.* with the solo part.) A direction to the accompanist
Colla voce		(*lit.* with the voice.) To follow the solo instrument or voice
Come	. .	As
Come prima	.	As at first
Come sopra	.	As above
Comodo	.	Convenient (usually linked with tempo—at a convenient pace)
Con	. .	With
Con sordino, ⎱ con sordini ⎰	.	With the mute, with the mutes
Contra Fagotto	.	Double Bassoon

Corda . . .	A string. See una corda, tre corde
Crescendo Cresc. } . .	Becoming gradually louder
Da . . .	From
Da capo D.C. } . .	From the beginning
Dal segno D.S. } . .	From the sign 𝄋
Deciso . . .	Decisively, firmly
Decrescendo Decresc. } . .	Becoming gradually softer
Delicato . .	Delicate
Dièse (*Fr.*) . .	The sharp sign (♯)
Diminuendo Dim. } . .	Becoming gradually softer
Divisi Div. } . .	A direction to orchestral players (usually strings) to divide into two or more groups
Dolce . . .	Tenderly, sweetly
Dolcissimo Dolciss. } . .	Very gently, very sweetly
Dolente . . .	Sadly
Dolore . . .	Grief, sorrow
Doppio . . .	Double
Doppio movimento .	Twice as fast
Duo . . .	A duet
Dur (*Ger.*) . .	Major (G dur: G major)
E, Ed. . . .	And
Ein wenig (*Ger.*)	A little
En dehors (*Fr.*) .	Prominently, *i.e.* emphasized
En pressant (*Fr.*) .	Hurrying
En retenant (*Fr.*) .	Gradually slower
Energico . .	With energy
Espressione . .	Expression

Espressivo Espr. Espress.	. .	With expression
Etwas (*Ger.*) . .	With expression	Somewhat
Facile . . .		Easy
Feurig (*Ger.*) .		Fiery
Finale . . .		The last movement of such a work as a Sonata
Fine . . .		The end
Forte *f*	. .	Loud
Forte piano *fp*	. .	Loud, then soft
Fortissimo *ff* or *fff*	. .	Very loud
Forza . . .		Force
Forzando *fz*	. .	Forcing, a sudden accent
Fuga . . .		A fugue
Fuoco . . .		Fire
Furioso . . .		Furiously
Gauche (*Fr.*) .		Left
Giocoso Giojoso	. .	Gay, merry
Giusto . . .		Strict, exact
(Tempo giusto	.	In strict time)
Glissando .	.	The rapid playing of a scale passage by drawing thumb or finger across the keys. A similar effect is possible across the strings of a harp, or by a portamento effect on a string of a violin or similar instrument ; or by manipulating the slide of a trombone

G.P. General Pause Grand Pause	.	Indicates to an orchestral player that he is to remain silent and that all the other players are silent as well.
Grandioso	. .	Grandly, in the grand manner
Grave	. . .	Very slow, solemn
Grazia	. . .	Grace
Grazioso	. .	Gracefully
H (*Ger.*)	. .	The note B natural.

Hence:

Immer (*Ger.*)	. .	Always, constantly
Impetuoso	. .	Impetuously

In alt . . . Notes from to

are said to be in alt

In altissimo	. .	Notes an octave higher than in alt
Incalzando	. .	Increasing speed, with often an implication of increasing tone
Lacrimoso	. .	(*lit.* tearfully.) Sadly
Lamentoso	. .	Mournfully
Langsam (*Ger.*)	.	Slow
Largamente	. .	Broadly
Larghetto	. .	Less slow than largo
Largo	. . .	Slow and stately
Lebhaft (*Ger.*)	.	Lively
Legato	. . .	Smooth
Legatissimo	. .	As smoothly as possible
Leggiero	. .	Light, delicate
Legno	. . .	See col legno
Lent (*Fr.*)	. .	Slow
Lento	. . .	Slow

L.H. (*Eng.*) . .		Left hand
Lied (*Ger.*) . .		Song
Lieder ohne Worte . (*Ger.*)		Songs without words (Mendelssohn)
L'istesso tempo .		(*lit.* the same speed.) The speed of the beat remains the same although the notation changes
Loco . . .		(*lit.* place.) Notes are to be played at their normal pitch (after an indication to play them an octave higher or lower)
Lontano . .		As from a distance
Lunga pausa . .		A long pause
Lusingando . .		In a coaxing style
Ma . . .		But
Ma non troppo .		But not too much
Maestoso . .		Majestically
Mancando . .		Waning, dying away
Main droite (*Fr.*)		
Mano destra	⎬	The right hand
M.D.		
Main gauche (*Fr.*)		
Mano sinistra	⎬	The left hand
M.G. or M.S.		
Marcato	⎬ . .	Marked, accented
Marc.		
Marcia . . .		A march
Martellato . .		Hammered out
Marziale . .		Martial
Mässig (*Ger.*) .		Moderate
Meno . . .		Less
Meno mosso .		Less movement, slower at once
Mesto . . .		Sadly
Mezza voce . .		(*lit.* half voice.) In an undertone

Mezzo forte} mf	. .	Moderately loud
Mezzo piano} mp	. .	Moderately soft
Misterioso	. .	Mysterious
Misura .	. .	(*lit.* measure.) Senza misura—in free time
Mit (*Ger.*)	. .	With
Moderato	. .	Moderate time
Moll (*Ger.*)	. .	Minor
Molto .	. .	Much. Di molto, very much
Morendo	. .	Dying away
Mosso .	. .	Moved, movement
Moto } Movimento	. .	Movement. Doppio movimento, twice as fast
MS. (*Eng.*)	. .	Manuscript
Muta .	. .	Change, *e.g.* Muta D in C is a direction to the Timpani player in the orchestra to tune the drum previously in D, to C
Nicht (*Ger.*)	. .	Not
Nobilmente	. .	Nobly. A term much used by Elgar
Non	. .	Not
Non tanto	. .	Not so much
Non troppo	. .	Not too much
Obbligato	. .	Indispensable, cannot be omitted
Opus (*Lat.*)	. .	A work. A published composition, *e.g.* Symphony No. 4 in E minor, Op. 98. Brahms
Ossia .	. .	Or. The word indicates an alternative version of a passage
Ostinato	. .	(*lit.* obstinate.) Frequently repeated : *e.g.* Basso ostinato : a composition in which a bass

tune (usually of 4 or 8 bars) is repeated with varied treatment at each repetition

Ottava / Ott. }	. .	Octave
Ottava bassa .	.	An octave lower
Parlando / Parlante }	. .	(*lit.* speaking.) To be sung in declamatory fashion with particular care for the enunciation of the words
Partitur (*Ger.*)	.	A full orchestral score
Passionato	. .	Passionately
Pastorale	. .	In a pastoral style
Patetico . .	.	With feeling, with pathos
Pausa . .	.	A rest (see G.P.)
Ped. . .	.	Depress the right (sustaining) pedal of the piano. The sign * means that the pedal should be released
Perdendosi .	.	Dying away
Pesante . .	.	Heavy, ponderous
Piacevole .	.	Pleasing, agreeable
Piangevole .	.	Plaintively
Piano / *p* }	. .	Soft
Pianissimo / *pp* or *ppp* }	.	Very softly
Più . .	.	More
Più allegro .	.	Quicker, more lively
Più lento .	.	More slowly
Più mosso .	.	More movement, quicker
Pizzicato / Pizz. }	. .	Plucked (in string music)
Plus (*Fr.*) .	.	More
Pochettino .	.	A very little

Pochissimo	. .	As small as possible
Poco	. . .	A little
Poco a poco	.	Little by little
Poi	. . .	Then
Ponticello	. .	The bridge of a violin or similar instrument. Sul ponticello is a direction to string players to play near the bridge
Portamento	. .	A term to express the effect produced on a stringed instrument or by the human voice in gliding with extreme smoothness from note to note
Precipitato Precipitoso	. .	Precipitately, impetuously
Prestissimo	. .	As fast as possible
Presto	. . .	Very quick
Prima volta	. .	First time (1ma volta)
Primo	. . .	First
Quasi	. . .	As if, almost
Quasi recitativo	.	Like a recitative
Quasi una fantasia	.	As if it were a fantasia, in the style of a fantasia
Rallentando Rall.	.	Becoming gradually slower
Repetizone Replica	.	Repetition
R.H. (*Eng.*)	. .	Right hand
Rigoroso	. .	Strictly
Rinforzando *rf.*	.	Reinforcing, *i.e.* increased tone on a single note or a small group of notes not strictly a sudden accent
Risoluto	. .	Resolute, bold
Risvegliato	. .	With increased animation

Ritardando Ritard }	.	Gradually slower
Ritenuto Rit. }	. .	Held back
Ritmico .	. .	Rhythmically
Rubato Tempo rubato }	.	Robbed, stolen, taking a portion of the duration from one note or group of notes and adding it to another, so that although the detail varies the length of the phrase is normal
Ruhig (*Ger.*) .	.	Calm
Scherzando .	.	Playful
Scherzo .	. .	A joke
Scherzoso .	.	Playfully
Schnell (*Ger.*) .	.	Quick
Schneller (*Ger.*)	.	Quicker
Sec .	. .	(*lit.* dry.) Detached
Segno .	. .	A sign (𝄋). See Dal segno
Segue .	. .	Go on with what follows
Sehr (*Ger.*) .	.	Very
Semplice .	.	Simple
Sempre .	. .	Always
Senza .	. .	Without
Senza sordini .	.	Without mutes (for string and brass players). See also Sordini
Sforzando Sforzato *sf, sfz* }	. .	Forcing, accented
Simile .	. .	In a like manner
Sin', Sino .	.	Until
Slargando Slentando }	.	Gradually slower

Smorzando	. .	Dying away
Soave	. .	Gentle, smooth
Solenne	. .	Solemn
Sonore	. .	Sonorous, full-toned
Sopra	. .	Above
Sordini	. .	Mutes. Con sordini : With mutes. A direction for string or brass players. Senza Sordini : (1) Without mutes (string and brass players). (2) For pianists, depress the "sustaining" pedal (thereby raising the dampers from the strings and permitting the strings to vibrate freely).
Sospirando	. .	Sighing
Sostenuto	. .	Sustained
Sotto	. .	Below
Sotto voce	. .	In an undertone
Spiccato	. .	Detached, with springing bow. (A direction for string players.)
Spiritoso	. .	Spirited
Staccato} Stacc. }	. .	Detached
Staccatissimo	. .	Very detached
Strepitoso	. .	Noisy, boisterous
Stringendo	. .	Gradually faster
Suave	. .	Gentle, smooth
Subito	. .	Suddenly
Sul	. .	On
Sul G	. .	On the G string (violin)
Süss (*Ger.*)	. .	Sweet
Sul ponticello	. .	Near the bridge (a direction to string players)
Tacet (*Lat.*)	. .	It is silent

Tanto	. . .	So much
Tasto Solo	. .	A term used in connection with figured bass to indicate that the bass part is to be played alone, without harmony
Tempo	. . .	The speed
Tempo comodo	.	At a convenient speed
Tempo giusto	.	In strict time
Tempo primo Tempo I (or I^mo)	}	Resume the original speed
Tempo rubato	. .	See Rubato
Tenerezza	.	Tenderness
Teneramente	.	Tenderly
Tenuto Ten.	} . .	Held
Tosto	. .	Swift, rapid
Tranquillo	.	Calm, tranquil
Traurig (Ger.)	.	Sadly
Tre	. .	Three
Tre corde	. .	(lit. three strings.) Release the left (soft) pedal of the pianoforte
Tremolando Tremolo Trem.	} .	The rapid repetition of a note (𝄐) or rapid alternation of two notes (♫)
Trionfale Trionfante	} . .	Triumphant
Troppo	. .	Too much
Tutta forza	.	The whole power, as loud as possible
Tutti	. .	All
Un, una, uno	.	One
Un peu (Fr.) Un poco	} .	A little

Una corda . .	.	(*lit.* one string.) In pianoforte music it indicates that the left (soft) pedal should be used
Unis. . .	.	Used in orchestral music, to show that the strings play in unison again after having been divided (divisi)
Veloce . .	.	Swift, quick
Vibrato . .	.	Vibrating
Vif (*Fr.*) .	.	Lively, quick
Vigoroso .	.	Boldly, vigorously
Vite (*Fr.*) Vivace Vivement (*Fr.*) Vivo	.	Quick, lively
Vivacissimo .	.	Very lively, with extreme vivacity
Voce . .	.	Voice
Volante .	.	Flying
Voll (*Ger.*) .	.	Full
Volti subito V.S.	.	Turn the page quickly
Wenig (*Ger.*) .	.	Little
Zart (*Ger.*) .	.	Delicate
Zu (*Ger.*) .	.	Too

MUSICAL FORMS

This list includes most of the musical forms that the student is likely to meet, and covers all that is required for Grade VIII. Certain technical terms that are connected with Form, such as Bridge Passage, Cadenza, Stretto are included, but it has all been made as concise as possible. For fuller information the student is referred to any good musical dictionary.

Abridged Sonata Form. Sonata Form in which the Development section is omitted, its place being taken by a short modulatory passage or even by a single chord of the dominant 7th.

Allemande. One of the normal movements in the 18th Cent. Suite. It is in $\frac{4}{4}$ time, only moderately quick, but with a good deal of semiquaver movement. It starts either with the last semiquaver, or with the last three semiquavers of a bar. Its form is Binary.

Anglaise. An English rustic dance, or what certain composers thought such a dance might be. It had no definite rhythmical pattern, except that it was in Simple time. A specimen occurs in Bach's 3rd French Suite.

Answer. The second entry of the theme in a Fugue, usually in the dominant key. It may be an exact transposition of the Subject, and is then called a Real Answer.

BACH '48' Book II Nº 9

Real Answer

Subject

Countersubject

But in certain circumstances it may be slightly modified to ease the relationship of tonality and is called a Tonal Answer.

BACH '48
Book II N⁰ 2
Tonal Answer
Subject
Countersubject

Aria.   A song, or song-like composition, usually in three-sections (Ternary) form.

Arietta.   An aria shortened by the omission of the middle section.

Augmentation.   The presentation of a theme, particularly in fugue, in notes of greater time-value than the original.

Bagatelle.   A short, unpretentious composition.

Ballad.   A song in which usually each verse is sung to the same tune.

Ballade.   A title given by certain composers, notably Chopin and Brahms to pieces of a romantic type, usually for a single instrument.

Barcarolle (*lit.* a boat-song).   A lyrical piece usually in compound time and ternary form.

Basso Ostinato.   See Ostinato.

Berceuse.   (i) A cradle song.   (ii) A quiet instrumental piece marked by persistant rocking movement.

Binary Form.   A Form in two sections, of which the first leads to an ending in a new Key, commonly dominant or relative major, and the second beginning in that new key and using the same material leads back to the original key.   Examples are found in most of the movements in the 18th Cent. Suites.

Bolero.   A lively Spanish dance in $\frac{3}{4}$ time using the rhythm

Bourrée.   A French dance in $\frac{2}{2}$ time, similar in style to the Gavotte, but faster and beginning on the last crotchet of the bar.

Bridge passage.   A transition in the exposition of Sonata Form (q.v.) to link the first subject (or subject-group) with the second.

Cadenza.   A passage occurring towards the end of a Concerto movement.   It is usually florid and brilliant, in order to show the technical skill of the performer. With few exceptions it is for the solo instrument alone without orchestra.

Canon.   A composition in which a theme announced by one part is, a short distance later, reproduced by another at a fixed interval higher or lower, the two parts continuing in this way throughout a movement, or section of a movement: *e.g.*, the last movement of Cesar Franck's Sonata for Violin and Piano, or the hymn-tune 'Tallis's Canon.'

Cantata.   A composition, sacred or secular for solo voices, chorus and orchestra.

Canto Fermo (*lit.* fixed song).   Usually a piece of plain song, but sometimes a secular tune sung in long note-values by the tenor and used as a basis for contra-puntal elaboration.

Canzona.   (i) A song.   (ii) In the 16th, 17th and 18th centuries a short instrumental piece in contrapuntal style.

Canzonet.   A little song, and particularly in the 16th and 17th centuries a piece in Madrigalian style for 2 or 3 voices.

Capriccio.   A caprice, free in form and light in style.

Catch.   A Round (q.v.) in which there is a play on words.

Cavatina.   A short piece of the ' aria ' type primarily for voices, but also a title for a short instrumental piece.

Chaconne.   A composition similar to the Passacaglia (q.v.)

Coda (*lit.* a tail).   A passage of greater or less length at the end of a movement to round it off more effectively.

Codetta.   (i) A small coda at the end of the Exposition of a movement in Sonata Form.   (ii) In Fugue, a link between entries of subject and answer in the Exposition.

Concertante.   A work for a group of solo instruments and orchestra, cf. Concerto Grosso.

Concerto.   A work usually in three movements for one or more solo instruments and orchestra.

Concerto Grosso.   A work for a group of soloists with orchestra :   *e.g.* Concerti grossi by Handel and other 18th century composers.   The soloists are termed ' concertante ' players, and the others ' ripieno.'

Concert Overture.   A detached work for orchestra, often with a ' programme ' and usually in Sonata Form.

Concertstück (*lit.* Concert-piece).   A piece in concerto style, but usually in only one movement :   *e.g.* Weber's Concertstück in F minor for piano and orchestra.

Corrente.   An Italian dance used in the 18th century Suite.   It is faster than the French Courante (q.v.) in regular triple time ($\frac{3}{4}$ or $\frac{3}{8}$) with constant use of running half-beat notes.   It is in Binary form.

Counter-exposition.   A second exposition in Fugue immediately following the first, but with the voices entering in a different order.

Counter-subject.   In a Fugue, the counterpoint with
which the first voice, having announced the Subject,
accompanies the Answer, and with which the second
voice accompanies the third voice and so on through
the exposition.   It sometimes accompanies subsequent
entries of the Subject and is then called a ' Regular
Counter-subject ' ; but such a thing is by no means an
invariable constituent of a Fugue.

Courante.   The French equivalent of the Corrente (q.v.).
It is somewhat slower and has more rhythmical variety
in that at Cadence points it commonly turns from $\frac{3}{2}$ to $\frac{6}{4}$.

Development-section.   See Sonata Form.

Diminution.   The writing of a theme in shorter note-
values than the original.

Double Counterpoint.   Two melodies so written that
they sound equally well when their relative positions
are reversed.

Double Fugue.   A Fugue on two subjects, which may be
announced together and worked together throughout,
or may be first worked separately and eventually
combined.

Ecossaise.   A Dance, nominally Scottish, in $\frac{3}{4}$ time, of
which Schubert wrote several examples.

Entr'acte.   (i) The interval between acts of an opera.
(ii) Music performed during that interval.

Episode.   (i) In Fugue, the passages that link entries of the
subject after the exposition: (ii) In Ternary or Rondo,
the contrasting sections between appearances of the
principal theme: (iii) In Sonata Form, new material
which sometimes appears in the development section.

Etude.   A Study : a work calculated to develop or display
the performer's technique.

Exposition.   The opening section of a composition in which the principal themes are first heard—in Sonata Form up to the end of the second subject together with any codetta that may follow : in Fugue up to the point when all the voices have entered and sung subject or answer once.

Fancy.   The Old English equivalent of the Fantasia, used by English composers of the 16th and 17th centuries as a title for pieces written for Virginals or for a ' Consort of Viols.'

Fantasia (*Ital.*).   Phantasie (*Germ.*)   Fantaisie (*French*). A movement in no specific form but in improvisatory style : often used as a prelude to another movement— *e.g.* a Fugue.

First Movement Form.   Another name for Sonata Form (q.v.).

Free Fantasia.   An alternative name for the Development Section in Sonata Form.

Fugato.   A piece in fugal style, but not showing the complete structure of a Fugue.

Fughetta.   A small Fugue, commonly lacking the ' middle section.'

Fugue.   Usually considered rather as a style of writing than as a form.   It is a contrapuntal piece founded on a theme, usually short, called the subject, and is written for two or more ' voices ' or parts.   For analytical purposes it is divided into three sections :—(i) Exposition, in which the parts enter in turn with alternately subject, in tonic key, and its transposed form (the answer) in dominant ; (ii) Middle section in which entries of subject and answer appear in keys other than those in the exposition, with episodes to link them and to effect the modulations ; (iii) Final Section, in which a return is made to tonic key and at least one entry of subject is heard in that key. But in practice once the exposition is complete there is no fixed procedure.

Various devices can be used, as the composer will, such as Augmentation, Diminution, Pedal-point, Stretto, all of which are described under their separate headings.

See also Double Fugue.

Galliard. An early dance in quick triple time, originally Italian, but much used in 16th and 17th century English works for the Virginals. It often followed a Pavan, which was sometimes preceded by a Prelude, thus forming an embryo Suite.

Gavotte. A French dance in dignified $\frac{2}{2}$ time, starting on the second half of a bar. Often followed by a second Gavotte, which sometimes took the form of a Musette (q.v.) the first Gavotte being repeated after the second.

Gigue. A lively dance in $\frac{6}{8}$ or $\frac{12}{8}$ time and in Binary form. It formed the last movement of the 18th century Suite. In Bach's Gigues each half is sometimes fugal with the second half built on an inversion of the theme of the first half.

Glee. A vocal piece for unaccompanied men's voices :— either serious or light in character. It was peculiar to England.

Ground Bass. A composition in which a short bass tune is repeated a number of times with varied treatment above it at each repetition c.f Ostinato.

Hornpipe. A lively dance of English origin, at first in triple time (see Handel's Water Music) but later in quadruple time.

Idyll. A composition of quiet, pastoral nature ; *e.g.* Wagner's Siegfried Idyll.

Imitation. The immediate reproduction, usually not quite exact, in a second part of a tune already heard in another part.

Impromptu. A piece suggestive of an improvisation : *e.g.* Impromptus by Schubert.

Intermezzo. (i) An interlude. (ii) A piece, usually for Piano, with no special characteristics.

Invention. A short contrapuntal piece built on one musical idea : *e.g.* two-part Inventions by Bach.

Jig. See Gigue.

Leitmotiv. A theme in an opera or a symphonic poem that represents a particular idea or character.

Loure. An old French dance in slow $\frac{6}{4}$ or occasionally $\frac{3}{4}$ time (see Bach's Third French Suite).

Madrigal. A contrapuntal composition for unaccompanied voices in from three to eight parts. Italian in origin, but much cultivated by 16th and early 17th century English composers, among them Byrd, Gibbons, Morley, Weelkes and Wilbye.

March. A strongly rhythmical piece in duple or quadruple time, apt for processional purposes.

Masque. A dramatic production which combined poetry, music and dancing, very popular in the 16th and 17th centuries, one of the most famous being Milton's Comus, produced at Ludlow Castle in 1634, with music by Henry Lawes.

Mazurka. A Polish dance in triple time with the second beat of the bar accented.

Minuet. A stately dance in $\frac{3}{4}$ time, commonly followed by a second Minuet, called a trio, after which the first is repeated.

Modified Sonata Form.   See abridged Sonata Form.

Motet.   A sacred choral composition in contrapuntal style, usually unaccompanied.

Moto Perpetuo.   An instrumental piece with a continuous flow of short, quick notes.

Musette.   (i) A species of bagpipes.   (ii) A piece of pastoral character on a drone bass, which sometimes follows a Gavotte (*e.g.* Bach's English Suite in G minor).

Nocturne (*lit.* a night piece).   A dreamy, lyrical piece for Piano originally produced by John Field and developed by Chopin.

Novelette.   A romantic movement, with no fixed form, first used by Schumann.

Octet.   Eight solo instruments or voices : or a composition for them.

Opera.   A play set to music, usually for solo voices, chorus and orchestra.   Grand Opera has music throughout, Light Opera includes a certain amount of spoken dialogue.

Oratorio.   A musical setting of a Biblical story for solo voices, chorus and orchestra.

Overture.   An orchestral introduction to an opera or oratorio.   Two special types of overture were used in the 18th century :   (1) The Italian Overture, used by Alessandro Scarlatti, was in three sections, a quick, a slow and a quick movement ;   (ii) The French form, associated with Lully and much used by Handel, had a slow first movement, usually repeated, a quick movement commonly in fugal style, and a stately dance movement to complete it.   See also Concert Overture.

Partita.   Usually synonymous with Suite, but sometimes denotes a set of Variations.

Passacaglia. A work built on a Ground Bass in slow triple time. The bass theme may be transferred to inner or upper parts and may be decorated. Examples for the organ by Bach and many other composers are to be found and the finale of Brahms's fourth Symphony is in this form.

Passepiéd. A quick dance in triple time, sometimes to be found in the Suite.

Pastorale. An instrumental piece of gently moving rhythm in $\frac{6}{8}$ or $\frac{12}{8}$.

Pavan. A stately—even solemn—dance in duple time which often preceded, and supplied the material for the Galliard (q.v.).

Pedal point. A sustained or repeated note, usually but not necessarily in the bass, on which the other parts continue moving with varied harmonies.

Polonaise or Polacca. A Polish dance in triple time and of moderate speed, but sounding quick and busy because of much repetition of notes and chords. The phrases end on the third beat of the bar.

Prelude. A piece suitable to serve as an introduction, e.g. to a Fugue, as in Bach's ' 48.' Often, however, a detached piece of romantic type. Many Preludes have been written for Piano, often in sets of twenty-four, e.g. by Chopin, Rachmaninoff, Scriabin and others.

Recapitulation. See Sonata Form.

Redundant Entry. An extra entry of the first voice, in Fugue, at the end of the Exposition.

Reel. A lively dance in $\frac{4}{4}$, or sometimes $\frac{6}{4}$ time, popular in Scotland and the North of England, but actually of Scandinavian origin.

Requiem. A Mass for the dead, set to music, *e.g.* by Palestrina and Victoria. In modern times extended settings with orchestra have been made by Berlioz, Dvorak, Fauré, Mozart and Verdi. Brahms's so-called Requiem is not a Mass, but a setting of certain passages from the German Bible.

Rhapsody. A work after the fashion of a Fantasia. Brahms and Dohnanyi amongst others have written such works for Piano.

Ricercare. A Fugue in which all the devices of subject treatment are exploited.

Rigaudon. An old French dance in lively duple or quadruple time, with some affinity to the Bourrée.

Ripieno. See Concerto Grosso.

Rondo. A composition in which a principal theme alternates with episodes on the plan A B A C A, in which A is the principal theme, and B and C the episodes. A more elaborate form of it—Sonata Rondo—was also used in which the Rondo principle is combined with Sonata Form, the plan being A B A C A B A. A is principal theme, B second theme, and C an episode.

Round. A canon at the unison for three or more voices: *e.g.* Three Blind Mice.

Sarabande. A slow dance in simple triple time with a stress on the second beat of the bar. A regular part of the 18th century Suite.

Scherzo (*lit.* a joke). An instrumental piece of a playful, sometimes of a grimly humorous character, quicker than but on the same plan as the Minuet and Trio. Sometimes a detached movement, but commonly a movement in Sonata or Symphony.

Siciliano.   A slow dance in $\frac{6}{8}$ or $\frac{12}{8}$ time.

Sonata.   Originally a word denoting instrumental music as opposed to Cantata, which was vocal ; but it was later limited to a work of some size, usually in three or four movements for one or two instruments.   Such works for more than two instruments are called Trios, Quartets, Quintets etc., and those for full orchestra are Symphonies.

Sonata Form.   The design commonly used in the Classical period, and often by later composers, for the First movement of a Sonata and so often called ' First Movement Form.'   It can also frequently be found in other works than Sonatas.   It has three main divisions :— (i) Exposition : a first subject, or group of subjects in tonic key, linked by a Bridge passage to a second subject, or group, in a related key, ending usually with a Codetta.   (ii) Development, in which material from the Exposition is treated in a variety of ways and occasionally new matter (Episode) is introduced.   (iii) Recapitulation ; a restatement of the Exposition material, but with the second subject in Tonic key, and sometimes with other modifications.   As with all movements this can, and usually does, end with a Coda.

Sonata Rondo.   See under Rondo.

Sonatina.   A small Sonata, often with fewer movements and those movements on a smaller scale than in a Sonata.

Stretto.   In Fugue, the Subject in Canon, *i.e.* a second voice entering with the subject before the previous entry is complete.   This device is common in, but not confined to, the final section of a fugue, often over a pedal-point.   When all the voices are involved in a stretto and all of them have complete entries of the subject, it is known as ' stretto maestrale."

Suite. A group of pieces. The Classical Suite consisted, except for a possible Prelude, entirely of dances, all in Binary form and usually all in the same key. The basic dances were Allemande, Courante, Sarabande and Gigue and a number of other movements such as Gavotte, Bourrée, Minuet, Passepied were sometimes added.

The modern Suite is more free, none of its movements need be in dance rhythm, nor in Binary form, and certainly they will not all be in one key.

Symphony. (i) An orchestral work on the same general plan as a Sonata, but on a larger scale. (ii) An instrumental prelude or interlude in a vocal piece.

Tarantella. A very lively dance in $\frac{6}{8}$ time, which originated in Italy.

Ternary Form. A structure in three main sections, the first being repeated, sometimes with modification, after the second.

Toccata (*Lat. toccara*, to touch). A work for a key-board instrument on one fixed plan, designed to display the technical skill of the player.

Trio. (i) Three performers. (ii) Music written for three performers. (iii) The middle section of a Minuet or a Scherzo, so called because it was originally written for three players.

Triple Counterpoint. Three melodic parts so contrived that they will produce a satisfactory effect in whatever order they are arranged.

INDEX

PRINTED BY COMPTON PRINTING LTD. AYLESBURY

THEORY OF MUSIC

A BOOK ON
RUDIMENTS AND THEORY OF MUSIC
– BASED ON THE SYLLABUS OF THE THEORY EXAMINATIONS –

This book on Rudiments and Theory of Music is planned on quite new lines. It contains eight chapters, which progressively cover the requirements of Grade I (Primary) to Grade VIII (Final).

The chapters are laid out in short numbered paragraphs which, together with a detailed index, a glossary of musical terms and forms, make for simplicity and ease of reference. The book is 7½" x 5", there are 150 pages and over 300 music examples.

QUESTIONS AND EXERCISES ON THEORY OF MUSIC
– WITH HINTS ON WORKING –
by William Cole

This series of books of Questions and Exercises on Theory of Music, with hints, is published in eight books — one for each grade.

The series is issued as a guide to the study of musical theory by graded steps, and contains hundreds of examples and specimen questions, with hints, to assist the student preparing for an examination.

GRADE I (Primary)	**GRADE V** (Higher)
GRADE II (Elementary)	**GRADE VI** (Intermediate)
GRADE III (Transitional)	**GRADE VII** (Advanced)
GRADE IV (Lower)	**GRADE VIII** (Final)

THEORY PAPERS

The actual examination papers are issued annually on 1st January in graded sets. Each set contains the three question papers of the particular grade set during the preceding year, and there is ample space for pupils' answers. Papers are available for seven years.

GRADE I (Primary)	**GRADE V** (Higher)
GRADE II (Elementary)	**GRADE VI** (Intermediate)
GRADE III (Transitional)	**GRADE VII** (Advanced)
GRADE IV (Lower)	**GRADE VIII** (Final)

THE FORM OF MUSIC
by William Cole

An up-to-date and clear outlook on musical form.

THE ASSOCIATED BOARD OF THE ROYAL SCHOOLS OF MUSIC